ROUTLEDGE LIBRARY EDITIONS:
SOCIOLOGY OF RELIGION

Volume 17

I0130692

VIOLENCE AND THE SACRED IN THE MODERN WORLD

VIOLENCE AND THE SACRED IN THE MODERN WORLD

Edited by
MARK JUERGENSMEYER

Routledge
Taylor & Francis Group

LONDON AND NEW YORK

First published in 1991 by Frank Cass and Company Ltd

This edition first published in 2019
by Routledge
2 Park Square, Milton Park, Abingdon, Oxon OX14 4RN

and by Routledge
52 Vanderbilt Avenue, New York, NY 10017

Routledge is an imprint of the Taylor & Francis Group, an informa business

© 1992 Frank Cass & Co. Ltd

British Library Cataloguing in Publication Data
A catalogue record for this book is available from the British Library

ISBN: 978-0-367-02386-7 (Set)
ISBN: 978-0-429-02545-7 (Set) (ebk)
ISBN: 978-0-367-03086-5 (Volume 17) (hbk)
ISBN: 978-0-367-03089-6 (Volume 17) (pbk)
ISBN: 978-0-429-02031-5 (Volume 17) (ebk)

Publisher's Note
The publisher has gone to great lengths to ensure the quality of this reprint but points out that some imperfections in the original copies may be apparent.

Disclaimer
The publisher has made every effort to trace copyright holders and would welcome correspondence from those they have been unable to trace.

VIOLENCE AND THE SACRED IN THE MODERN WORLD

Edited by

MARK JUERGENSMEYER

FRANK CASS

First published 1991 in Great Britain by
FRANK CASS AND COMPANY LIMITED
Gainsborough House, 11 Gainsborough Road,
London E11 1RS, England

Copyright © 1992 Frank Cass & Co. Ltd

British Library Cataloguing in Publication Data

Violence and the sacred in the modern world.
  I. Juergensmeyer, Mark II. Journal of terrorism
  & political violence
  261.83

ISBN 0-7146-34565

Library of Congress Cataloging-in-Publication Data

Violence and the sacred in the modern world /
  edited by Mark Juergensmeyer.
  p.   cm.
  This group of studies first appeared in a special
  issue, Terrorism and political violence, vol. 3, no. 3'
  – T.p. verso.
  Includes bibliographical references (p.   ) and index.
  ISBN 0-7146-3456-5
  1. Violence – Religious aspects. 2. Terrorism –
  Religious aspects.
  I. Juergensmeyer, Mark.
  BL65.V55V56 1992
  291.5'697 – dc20   91-30464   CIP

This group of studies first appeared in a Special Issue:
The Journal of Terrorism and Political Violence Vol.
3, No. 3 published by Frank Cass & Co. Ltd.

Printed in Great Britain by Antony Rowe Ltd

Contents

Editor's Introduction:
Is Symbolic Violence Related
to Real Violence?

MARK JUERGENSMEYER

Violence has always been endemic to religion. Images of destruction and death are evoked by some of religion's most popular symbols, and religious wars have left through history a trail of blood. The savage martyrdom of Husain in Shiite Islam, the crucifixion of Jesus in Christianity, the sacrifice of Guru Tegh Bahadur in Sikhism, the bloody conquests in the Hebrew Bible, the terrible battles in the Hindu epics, and the religious wars attested to in the Sinhalese Buddhist chronicles indicate that in virtually every tradition images of violence occupy as central a place as portrayals of non-violence. This raises two haunting questions: why are these images so central, and what is the relationship between symbolic violence and the real acts of religious violence that occur throughout the world today?

To explore questions such as these, the Harry Frank Guggenheim Foundation convened an exploratory conference of scholars at Sterling Forest, New York, in September 1989. Most of those taking part were social scientists and scholars of comparative religion who have studied incidents of religious violence and terror caused by militant Muslims, Jews, Christians, Sikhs and Sinhalese Buddhists. One scholar, however, brought a more theoretical and literary perspective to these contemporary cases. This scholar, René Girard, has formulated theories about the social role of symbolic religious violence that have been widely discussed in his own field of comparative literature and throughout the humanities; they have been especially influencial in the field of religious studies. But despite the wide readership that his ideas have attracted, Girard has rarely come face to face with social scientists and other investigators of cases of religious violence in modern society. One of the significant moments in the conference was the dialogue among Girard and these scholars over the applicability of his theories to the contemporary world.

The dialogue that began at Sterling Forest continued in written form in 1990, culminating in a series of essays written by several of the participants on the relevance of Girardian themes to their own analyses of contemporary cases of religious violence. It is these essays, with Girard's written response, that are presented in this volume. The essays contain much more than a discussion of Girard – one will find useful information and penetrating analyses of a variety of situations in contemporary Lebanon, Israel, Egypt, Sri Lanka, India, Indonesia, and elsewhere – yet the themes that Girard has enunciated tie together the disparate interests of the authors.

The authors gratefully acknowledge the support of the Harry Frank Guggenheim Foundation for launching them on this venture, and the involvement of its president, James Hester, and its program officer, Karen Colvard, in the lively discussions that led to this book. Although this volume was not commissioned by the Foundation, nor does it contain the papers prepared for the 1989 conference in their original form, the conversation which the conference stimulated is appropriate to the Foundation's primary concern: understanding, and ameliorating, the forces that lead to conflict and violence in the contemporary age.

The Girardian Themes: Sacrifice and Mimetic Desire

Perhaps one of the reasons that Girard is regarded with such interest, especially in the field of Religious Studies, is that he supplies a straight-forward answer to a question that has vexed thoughtful observers of religion for centuries: why violence is so central to religion. In looking for an answer, Girard turns toward certain aspects of human relations that are potentially violent, and suggests that religion provides mechanisms for defusing their violence.[1]

In saying that violent symbols and sacrificial rituals evoke, and thereby vent, violent impulses, Girard follows the lead of Sigmund Freud, who also wrote about the importance that religion holds in symbolically displacing feelings of hostility and violence. Freud is, in fact, the major theorist with whom Girard wrestles in his pioneering theoretical work, *Violence and the Sacred*, and Girard is sometimes congratulated for rescuing an interesting Freudian explanation for religious violence from its ties to the controversial theory of the Oedipal complex.

Similar to Freud, Girard is fascinated with religious myths of violence and sacrificial rites. Girard, like his famous mentor, regards such myths and rituals as recollections of original violent acts that must be controlled. Girard and Freud both regard these incidents and their symbolic responses as ubiquitous in religious traditions; understanding them is critical to an understanding of the meaning of religion *per se*. If one can decipher their importance for the human condition, one can understand what lies behind religion; and in doing that one deciphers the puzzle behind all forms of culture.

Common to both Freud and Girard is the notion that sacrifice is the primary sacred act. It is primary, they assert, because those who conduct a rite of sacrifice are projecting onto the sacrificial victim qualities that relate to some of their own most intimate concerns. In demolishing the victim they are symbolically annihilating aspects of themselves. What is destroyed is destructiveness itself: the feelings of violence and hostility that lie behind attempts to carry out violent activities. Such feelings are antithetical to the ties of friendship that bond a community together, and feelings of violence toward one's peers and associates must be banished if a closely-knit community – such as a tribal brotherhood, a spiritual fellowship, or a modern nation – is to survive.

Insofar as sacrifice is a mechanism for helping to banish intra-communal violence, it plays an important social role, one which both Freud and Girard see as positive. It allows adherents to release feelings of hostility towards members of their own communities, thereby 'purifying' these feelings and allowing for the social cohesion of affinity groups. 'The function of ritual', claims Girard, 'is to "purify" violence; that is, to "trick" violence into spending itself on victims whose death will provoke no reprisals'.[2] Of course, those who participate in rituals of violence are not consciously aware of the social and psychological significance of their acts, for indeed 'religion tries to account for its own operation metaphorically'.[3]

Thus far, Girard and Freud are in agreement, but Girard parts company with Freud over the question of what causes these destructive urges. Freud, in a famous hypothesis extracted from the myth of Oedipus, suggests that instincts of sexuality and aggression aimed at parental figures lie behind the desire to destroy, and these are the traits projected onto the scapegoat foe. Girard rejects this, and attributes the root cause of violence to what he terms 'mimetic desire'.

Mimetic desire, according to Girard, is 'a desire imitated from the desire of a model who thereby runs the risk of becoming a rival for the same object of desire'.[4] One identifies with an idealized image of another person. Yet this identification can also lead to competition and hatred of the other. For this reason, posits Girard, it is important to have symbols of the rival that one can conquer, and therefore assimilate. Hence the centrality of the rite of sacrifice: it offers up a scapegoat of the rival that one can literally devour. It thereby fulfills not only the cultural and community-building functions that Freudian theory implies, but also personal goals, such as controlling one's feelings of competition and aggression. Without it, mimetic desire can run amok, and violent urges can become focused on scapegoat enemies rather than on symbolic victims. Such is the situation a society confronts when it no longer has convincing symbols of sacrifice to dispel violence. The society then faces a 'sacrificial crisis', as Girard puts it.

The two central aspects of Girard's theory – sacrifice and mimetic desire – are regarded by him as inextricably linked. But they are conceptually distinct. One can appreciate much of what Girard has to say about the function of sacrifice in symbolically displacing feelings of violence without accepting that mimetic desire is the villain that motivates the feelings. Similarly, one may see how mimetic desire plays a potent role in situations of conflict without looking for evidence of sacrificial displacement or even a 'sacrificial crisis' – the situation of violence that occurs when rituals are inadequate to displace violent urges.

In some of Girard's later writings there is yet a third aspect to his theory: the uniqueness of Christianity. According to Girard, among the world religions Christianity is alone in its understanding of the sacrificial victim. Nowhere else is God perceived as having played this role. Christ provides all humanity with a 'perfect model': one who, having no appropriate desire, does not run the risk of triggering mimetic rivalry.[5] He thereby ends the cycle of sacrifice by allowing himself to be the sacrificial victim. As a result Christianity gives to the world an enduring message of pathos and peace. Like other aspects of Girard's theory, however, one can accept or reject this aspect of it without disturbing the rest of his theoretical design.

Looking at Contemporary Cases of Real Religious Violence

What, one might ask, do these various aspects of Girard's theory have to do about *real* acts of religious violence in the contemporary world? The death squads of Sikh and Sinhalese revolutionaries, the Muslim terrorists of Lebanese and Egyptian movements, and the extreme elements of militant Jewish and Christian activists are all engaged in violence in a direct and significantly non-symbolic way. It might appear that their actions do not fit Girard's theories: their sacrifices do not result in the peaceful displacement of violence that ritualized forms of religious violence are supposed to produce, nor are Christian activists less vicious than religious warriors of other faiths. Yet it is the conviction of most contributors to this volume that some of Girard's ideas about symbolic violence can be applied to these real cases as well, making symbol and reality not so removed from one another as first they might appear.

The essays in this book explore Girardian themes in relation to real contemporary cases. Each of the authors has taken Girard seriously as an analyst of sacrificial violence, and they have looked at their own case studies to see which of Girard's theories apply. Some of the authors have found quite a bit of correspondence between what Girard says about symbolic religious violence and what occurs in the real world. Others have found less. In both cases they differ in what they regard as Girard's most significant contribution: some have found the notion of mimetic desire to be Girard's most suggestive idea; others have found to be more appealing his understanding of the role of sacrifice in displacing violence. Still others have replaced parts of Girard's theories with other theories, or found that his work, to be appreciated, must be understood in a broader theoretical context.

Among the authors in this volume, Mark Anspach, in 'Violence Against Violence: Islam in Comparative Context', has made the greatest use of Girard's theories. After looking at a number of instances of violence in pre-state societies, Anspach concludes that, like many traditional cultures, Islamic communities often resort to vendetta and punishment to deal with expressions of violent feelings, rather than relying solely on the mechanism of sacrificial ritual. He agrees with Girard that such a situation can create 'a sacrificial crisis', where ritual is confused with history. Without an adequate sacrificial lamb, violence is pitted against violence, as Girard has sometimes said, in a spiral of reprisals. The violence of contemporary Islam shows what happens when the mechanism of sacrifice does not work.

Martin Kramer, in 'Sacrifice and Fratricide in Shiite Lebanon', is also concerned with the sacrificial motif in contemporary Islamic violence. Kramer focuses on the recent cases of 'self-sacrifice' of those young members of the Hizbollah and Amal terrorist groups in Lebanon who have given their lives in suicide missions aimed against the American and Israeli military. What Kramer has found is that these young people bear many of the characteristics of sacrificial victims in traditional religion: they are physically and spiritually pure and yet in some ways socially marginal. They are of marriageable age, for instance, but not yet married; and some lack family ties. Kramer concludes that these agents of 'self-sacrifice' are in fact chosen by society, or at least by social pressure: they are victims. He goes on to claim that there is a sacrificial competition between the Hizbollah and Amal groups, creating what amounts to a 'mimetic rivalry' as each attempts to outdo one another in acts of self-sacrifice.

It is not Girard's notions of sacrifice, but his ideas about mimetic desire that initially interest Ehud Sprinzak in his essay, 'Violence and Catastrophe in the Theology of Rabbi Meir Kahane: The Ideologization of Mimetic Desire'. Here Sprinzak examines the writings of one of modern Israel's most strident religious ideologues, and finds within the late rabbi's thinking a pattern of mimetic rivalry, involving a desire to be like the Gentiles and to supersede them. The main purpose of God's creation of Israel, according to Kahane, is vengeance: to be a 'fist in the face of the Gentile world'. Yet Kahane rejects the symbolism of sacrifice that might (in Girard's reckoning) save Israel from the violent implications of this mimetic desire. According to Kahane, Israel must repudiate the sacrificial role that history – and the Hebrew Bible – would seem to force upon it. It must not be the willing lamb. But in abandoning the image of sacrifice, Kahane loses one of the resources that Judaism offers for symbolically displacing violence. As Girard's theory would leave one to conclude, Kahane is left with a strategy for confrontation that is based on vengeance, power, and violence. His is mimetic rivalry in its most raw form.

The theme of mimetic desire is also explored by Emmanuel Sivan in 'The Mythologies of Religious Radicalism: Judaism and Islam'. The rivalry that interests Sivan is the curious one in the Middle East between fundamentalist Muslims and fundamentalist Jews. Although they are, in a sense archenemies, the conservatives aim their arrows of degradation at the apostates in their own religious communities rather than at their Muslim or Jewish counterparts. In certain ways they seem to respect and even emulate one another. The Muslim censuring of Salman Rushdie, for example, was met with a certain approval by orthodox Jews; and Sivan implies that in many ways they compete in their attempts to out-orthodox each other. The sacrificial consequences of this mimetic desire are also noted by Sivan. He quotes a Jewish rabbi as having suggested that the *Intifada* could be handled by Israel sacrificing 'a scapegoat' – in this case, the Gaza strip – in order that bloodshed might be avoided.

The last three essays in the book take a somewhat different tack. Rather than applying aspects of Girard's themes to specific cases, they use these cases to evaluate some of Girard's basic assumptions. Bruce Lawrence, in 'The Islamic Idiom of Violence: A View from Indonesia', deduces from his study of the Indonesian case that what might appear to be religious violence in many parts of the world is in fact political violence. It is a part of (or a rejection of) the violence implicit in the construction of the modern nation-state. Taking cues from the British sociologist Anthony Giddens, Lawrence finds that Islam occupies a subordinate role in the modern world, and the violence attributed to it is in fact an aspect of modern nationalism. In Lawrence's view, Girard's theory, which initially emerged from the analysis of classical literary images, is not so much wrong in its own terms as irrelevant to the modern social situation.

My article, 'Sacrifice and Cosmic War', based on insights gleaned from case studies of Sikhs in India, Sinhalese Buddhists in Sri Lanka, Christians in Nicaragua, and Muslims and Jews in the Middle East, also questions some of Girard's assumptions. I begin, however, by agreeing with him in many basic respects. I concur that ritualized violence is important to virtually all religious cultures, and that violence conducted by religious actors in the real world often exploits those images. I question, however, the necessity of the concept of mimetic desire for explaining the origins of these symbols, and the notion that sacrifice is the fundamental religious image. Instead, it seems to me, a case may be made that what stands behind virtually all religious activity is the quest for order. This quest involves a struggle between order and disorder that is often exemplified in the grand metaphor of cosmic warfare. Sacred war is a dominant motif in the rhetoric of modern-day religious activists engaged in violent endeavors, and this metaphor, I suggest, is more seminal to their thinking than sacrifice.

David C. Rapoport's essay is not so much an application of Girard's theory, nor a critique – although he is disappointed at Girard's failure adequately to deal with the conscious use of violence by religious actors – as it is an attempt to put Girard in context. In 'Some General Observations on Religion and Violence', Rapoport outlines five reasons to think that religious revivals will always be associated with violence. The first has to do with the capacity of religion to command loyalties and enlist total commitment – a line of reasoning that is employed by political theorists, including Machiavelli. The second, which incorporates my point of view, focuses on the language of religion and the way that it is by its nature suffused with violence and images of sacred war. The third reason – which encapsulates Girard's perspective – emphasizes the violent origins of religion, and the aspects of these origins that help to keep violence in check. The fourth reason, the study of the role of revivalist and apocalpytic doctrines in fomenting religious violence, is the one with which Rapoport himself is most closely identified. A fifth reason stresses the connections betwen religious and political communities and the lure of religion for the secular political actor. In presenting each of these reasons, Rapoport draws on a variety of sources, and suggests that many of these points of view are more compatible and intersecting than they may first appear.

At the conclusion of the book, Girard himself has an opportunity to respond. In doing so he confronts some of the theoretical challenges made directly by the contributors to this volume and indirectly in the case studies to which they refer. Girard restates and defends many of his basic positions, and shows their relevance to contemporary issues.

Yet at the end of the book the reader is faced with many of the same questions with which the book began. Among them is a central one: does an understanding of the origins of the symbols of religious violence help in understanding actual instances of religious violence in the modern world?

The essays in this book do not give a definitive answer. They do not prove that Girard's theory is intrinsically true or consistently useful; nor do they prove the opposite. They do demonstrate, however, that in some cases, aspects of Girard's theory are not only useful but directly applicable. And in all cases they demonstrate that the themes that have exercised Girard's imagination – the motifs of sacrifice, rivalry and religious violence – are of enduring, and pointedly contemporarary, concern.

NOTES

1. The major work to which the authors of this volume refer is René Girard, *Violence and the Sacred*, trans. by Patrick Gregory (Baltimore; MD and London: The Johns Hopkins University Press, 1977), orig. published as *La Violence et le Sacre* (Paris: Editions Bernard Grasset, 1972). See also his *'To Double Business Bound': Essays on Literature, Myth, Mimesis, and Anthropology* (Baltimore, MD and London: The Johns Hopkins Press, 1978); *Things Hidden Since the Foundation of the World* (Stanford, CA: Stanford University Press, 1987), orig. published as *Des Choses Cachées depuis la Fondation du Monde: Recherches avec Jean-Michel Oughourlian et Guy LeFort* (Paris: Grasset, 1978); *The Scapegoat*, trans. by Yvonne Freccero (Baltimore, MD and London: The Johns Hopkins University Press, 1986), orig. published as *Le Bouc Emissaire* (Paris: Grasset, 1985); and *Job: The Victim of His People* (Stanford, CA: Stanford University Press, 1987), orig. published as *La Route Antique des Hommes Pervers: Essais sur Job* (Paris: Grasset, 1985); and Walter Burkhert, René Girard, and Jonathan Z. Smith, *Violent Origins: Ritual Killing and Cultural Formation*, edited by Robert G. Hamerton-Kelly (Stanford, CA: Stanford University Press, 1987).
2. Girard, *Violence and the Sacred*, p.36.
3. Girard, *Violence and the Sacred*, p.36.
4. Correspondence to me from Girard in response to an earlier draft of this introduction (4 Feb. 1991).
5. The wording in this description of Christ as 'perfect model' was provided by Girard (correspondence to me in response to an earlier draft of this introduction, 4 Feb. 1991).

Violence Against Violence:
Islam in Comparative Context

MARK R. ANSPACH

To study violence within religion is to confront a paradox, the definition of which depends on one's perspective. From a vantage point inside the Western religious tradition, religion may be perceived as inherently antithetical to violence, making religious violence a paradox from the point of view of the religion itself. But an observer surveying religions in general will find that such an internally-recognized antithesis is far from universal. For this outside observer, the real paradox is that religion can play a vital role in controlling violence *without* being antithetical to it. Indeed, from this point of view, the role of violence in religion constitutes perhaps the central paradox not only of religion but of social order itself.

In this article I explore the nature and implications of this paradox, focusing for the most part on the place of violence in the religious of 'primitive' or pre-state societies. Ritual sacrifice is the one kind of violence we all identify as religious since it has no apparent secular function. My argument is largely devoted to showing that other violent institutions that are not generally regarded as primarily religious – vendettas, leadership battles, the punishment of transgressors – can in pre-state societies be understood as extensions of sacrificial ritual which, together with sacrifice proper, form a unified system. I address the question of violence in a non-Western 'world religion', Islam, within the comparative context established by the preceding discussion.

Durkheim identified religion with the principle of social cohesion, and social cohesion requires in turn that a check be imposed on the centrifugal force of social violence. René Girard's contribution has been to demonstrate the paradox that religion controls violence *through* violence – it 'contains' violence in both senses of the word, employing 'good' violence against 'bad'. 'Good' violence is the controlled, inoculatory dose of violence directed against a scapegoat held responsible for the outbreak of uncontrolled 'bad' violence that like a plague threatens to engulf society. Religious ritual re-enacts the transition from the undifferentiated state of generalized violence to the differentiated state of social order through the sacrifice of a victim by the group. The opposition between the victim and the group is the primordial cultural difference; it is the foundation of the religiously sanctioned system of differences that defines the culture.

Differences keep the peace. This may seem an odd notion when we are accustomed to the language of 'overcoming differences', but it follows from Girard's observation that imitation – the attempt to be the 'same as' – leads to conflict if it is allowed to extend to the realm of desire: 'Two desires converging on the same object are bound to clash'.[1] In pre-state societies, individuals are assigned different objects by kinship regulations, 'totemic' obligations and prohibitions and what might be called the 'ritual division of labor'. In fact, as the anthropologist A. M. Hocart emphasized, where economic division of labor, and Durkheim's 'organic solidarity', are lacking, the 'only differentiation of function is in the ritual'.[2] It would be misleading to speak of the economy – or the family, or politics – as independent spheres of activity in a pre-state society, since not only are all these interrelated, they are also organized within a common religious framework. Religion furnishes the Durkheimian web of social cohesion, but it does this in the first place by forging differences; in the words of Lucien Scubla, 'religion indeed contributes to weaving the social bond, but it unites men by separating them, by putting them at a good distance from one another and by keeping them from getting too close to each other'.[3]

The first part of what religion achieves is to avoid occasions for friction. This is not to say that primitive religion eliminates all freedom of choice and hence all possibility of competition. Even the most rigidly prescriptive kinship system will not tell a man exactly whom to wed. Nonetheless, by defining a relatively narrow category, it significantly limits the potential for conflict.

We can reformulate this first aspect of religion in positive terms by saying that it channels rivalry into different directions. That is what it does day in and day out. On periodic occasions, however, there is a ceremonial reversal of the usual taboos that culminates with the channeling of violence in a single direction. After being kept apart the rest of the year, people are brought together at last around the same object – but only by sharing in its destruction. Nothing generates 'collective effervescence' like a well-organized lynching. As we know, the fundamental rite for Girard is the unanimous murder of a lone victim.

The unanimity of the group and the marginal status of the victim are essential to ensure that no one will come forward to wreak vengeance on the sacrificers. The sacrifice must remain an isolated act. Isolation of violence is the whole point of the procedure. Like desire, violence is contagious; sacrificial violence is 'good' violence insofar as it does not spread. The problem with vengeance, Girard writes, is that it 'threatens to involve the whole social body' because it is an 'interminable, infinitely repetitive process' of violence hurled against violence: 'every reprisal calls for another reprisal', and the 'multiplication of reprisals instantaneously puts the very existence of a society in jeopardy' – which, he concludes, 'is why it is universally proscribed'.[4]

Some anthropologists have challenged this vision of vengeance as a phenomenon whose appearance automatically places the society in mortal danger. Raymond Verdier points out that while vengeance is always proscribed among the members of a group, it becomes a social obligation in the face of aggression. Avenging the victim is a sacred duty for the survivors, often a religious duty sanctioned by the authority of spirits. Verdier's collaborator, Joseph Chelhod, describes the Bedouin belief that a murder victim's soul 'is transformed into a screech-owl who clamors incessantly to drink his enemy's blood'.[5] Little wonder that the quest for revenge takes priority over everything else. 'So that he would not be tempted to evade this sacred duty, the anteislamic Arab solemnly swore to renounce profane pleasures and the enjoyments of this world as long as he had not accomplished his vengeance.'[6]

Girard is of course aware that vengeance can be a duty; more than that, he sees here once again the paradox that violence can only be controlled through violence: 'The obligation never to shed blood cannot be distinguished from the obligation to exact vengeance on those who shed it'.[7] Verdier observes, however, that this duality is normally correlated with a distinction between aggressors from within the group and those from without: 'the duty of vengeance without is the counterpart of the prohibition on vengeance within: duty and prohibition express the two faces, external and internal, of solidarity; one cannot avenge oneself on those whom one has precisely the duty to avenge'.[8]

Not only is vengeance theoretically limited to dealing with offenders from the outside, its proper execution is typically governed by a host of other restrictions, leading Verdier to speak of it as a full-fledged 'system of regulation and social control having its rules and its rites' concerning the time, place, methods and targets of revenge. The kind of vengeance run wild that Girard depicts can only emerge when the system is not functioning: 'It is only when the system comes unhinged . . . or when it doesn't yet apply (as during the three days of the "boiling of the blood" after a deliberate murder, among the Bedouins) that vengeance goes wild'.[9] Verdier's own volumes are studded with sufficient fearsome examples of 'system failure' that we may suppose the threat of uncontrolled vengeance to be real enough.

It is clear, though, from his work and that of others, that the repetitive process of reprisals in a regulated vendetta may continue for generations without proving fatal to the society as a whole. Ernest Gellner recalls the astonishment of a field-worker observing negotiations for the settlement of a feud in southern Arabia upon learning 'that one of the deaths had been caused by an arrow – a weapon not in use in the region for a long, long time. In other words, the accountancies of reciprocal killing stretched back right into an age of long-past military technology, without straining anyone's arithmetic'. Still, while this suggests to Gellner 'an economical and relatively humane system', he cautions that at 'other times and places, feuds could escalate uncontrollably'.[10]

The stability of the feud requires that the adversary groups adhere to the same system of codes and rites. For this reason, a simple, twofold distinction between external and internal violence is inadequate. Verdier proposes a threefold distinction that situates vengeance in an 'intermediate social space' where the social distance between the parties involved is neither so small that it is forbidden nor so large that the conditions for its controlled application do not exist. In the world beyond the sphere of vengeance, the alterity of the other is 'such that any kind of recognition is ruled out and, for want of mediation, the affirmation of one party takes place through the negation of the other'. This is where vengeance gives way to war. While acknowledging that the two are often difficult to distinguish in practice,[11] Verdier stresses that the objective of vengeance is ideally restoration of parity among approximate equals rather than conquest or annihilation of an enemy; feuding parties seek to surpass but not destroy one another, defining each other through 'antagonistic complementarity' in a 'dynamic equilibrium'.[12]

The maintenance of a violent equilibrium among groups is itself a means of assuring the internal cohesion of each group. In his controversial reflections on Amerindian social structure, Pierre Clastres went so far as to present this type of chronic external violence as a way for tribal entities innocent of political inequality to keep the specter of coercive authority at bay: 'Primitive society is society against the State insofar as it is society-for-war'.[13] Alfred Adler notes a recent parallel tendency of some Africanists to treat endemic armed conflict as integral to the autonomous existence of the groups involved rather than as necessarily orientated towards territorial or other material aims.[14]

One need not see this form of violence as directed against the state to conceive it as an alternative to state organization. Expanding on the classic work of E. E. Evans-Pritchard, Gellner writes that, in egalitarian Muslim desert tribes lacking a central enforcement agency, order is maintained thanks to their segmentary social organization characterized

by the institution of the feud:[15]. 'The system works, without the benefit
of political centralization, through the cohesion-prompting presence of
violence at all levels'.[16] Segmentary groups are in horizontal juxtapo-
sition and vertically nested so that at each level are found rival groups
which are themselves subdivided into rival groups. Groups opposed at
one level will nonetheless cooperate in defending the larger group to
which they belong from a rival at the next level,[17], a pattern reflected
in the Arab aphorism 'I against my brothers, my brothers and I against
our cousins, my brothers, cousins and I against the world'.[18]

'The unifying effect of external threat is something which of course
operates in all societies', Gellner comments, but in segmentary societies,
he asserts, it is the dominant operating principle, 'or very nearly the only
one'.[19] At this point we may ask whether Gellner is not overlooking
a second and perhaps related principle at work in stateless societies
– namely, the unifying effect of sacrifice, with which we began. In
both cases exists the paradox of violence controlled through violence.
Whether the violence is channeled outwards, towards a member of an
external group, or inwards, towards a marginal member of the group
who is isolated and made external, it is prevented from spreading within
the group's own ranks.

Moreover, if the obligation of external vengeance is necessarily
accompanied by a ban on internal vengeance, internal offenses can only
be met with sacrificial measures. Either a purificatory rite is performed
to cleanse the group of the pollution created by the transgression, or
the transgressor is himself ritually expelled by and from the group.
The Cheyennes did both, as A. Hoebel tells us in a passage of *The
Law of Primitive Man* worth reproducing here for the enthusiasm with
which it underscores the opportunity for cohesion-building provided by
a murder within the tribe, an enthusiasm which can only be described
as infectious:

> . . . extrusion was necessary to cleanse the putrid infection from
> the body politic. The solution was exile . . . . Simple banishment of
> the offender was not enough, however. The tribe as well as the man
> was stained. Purification was called for, and this was done through
> the ritual of Renewal of the Medicine Arrows . . . . And by means
> of it the Cheyennes achieved a positive social result of tremendous
> value. As an integrator of the tribe nothing equaled it. The feeling
> of oneness was not to be escaped. So it was that the act which could
> shatter the unity of the tribe – homicide – was made the incident
> that formally reinforced the integrity of the people as a people.[20]

In ancient Hawaii the purification necessitated by a transgression of the taboos entailed the sacrifice of the transgressor himself. So conscious were the Hawaiians of the unequaled value of such proceedings that they sometimes were not content to wait for an offense to be committed. 'Transgressions are often artificially provoked when a sacrifice is necessary', explains Valerio Valeri, citing the account of an early nineteenth-century voyager: 'Taboos were instituted, such as it were next to impossible to observe, and the first offender was seized and dragged to the morair [temple] for sacrifice'.[21]

Hawaiian society included a special class of future sacrificial victims, the *kauwa*, considered the family gods of the nobles with whom they maintained a close relationship. This class comprised not only transgressors and rebels against the king, but also enemies taken prisoner.[22] Here one is reminded of those Amazonian Indians who used to integrate captives into society, give them a wife and treat them royally until the day they were sacrificed and eaten, a practice faithfully depicted in the film *How Tasty was My Little Frenchman*.

Just as Valeri views the Hawaiian taboos as a ritual device designed to guarantee an internal supply of victims, Girard sees the constant warfare of the Brazilian Tupinamba as a way of arranging a steady external source of victims: 'it can be said that the tribes have come to an agreement never to agree; that a permanent state of war is maintained for the express purpose of providing victims for ritual cannibalism'.[23] 'A sacrificial cult based on war and the reciprocal murder of prisoners is not substantially different from nineteenth-century nationalistic myths with their concept of an "hereditary enemy"', remarks Girard. 'In both instances the basic function of foreign wars, and of the more or less spectacular rites that generally accompany them, is to avert the threat of internal dissension by adopting a form of violence that can be openly endorsed and fervently acted upon by all'.[24]

Along with the foreign captives adopted into the group, the native warriors sent to die abroad may also be conceived of as a category of sacrificial victims. The latter aspect of fighting in pre-state societies is the one most clearly preserved in contemporary wars which no longer openly feature the murder of prisoners, but in which calls to sacrifice oneself in battle are often heard. The sacrificial status of the warrior is highlighted by Alfred Adler. Where Girard compares the lavishly received Tupinamba prisoner to the African sacred king, another marginal member of the community destined for ritual killing,[25] Adler draws an analogy between the African king and the Indian warrior of the Americas, portrayed by Clastres as engaged in an enterprise which can only be crowned with death:[26] 'Each feat of arms hailed and celebrated by the tribe in fact obligates him to aim higher',[27] until, 'realizing the supreme exploit, he thereby obtains, with absolute glory, death'.[28]

The ultimate feat according to Clastres is that of the warrior who heads off by himself to attack the enemy camp, braving 'the most absolute inequality': *'Alone against all . . .'*.[29] Clastres' absolute inequality corresponds to Girard's original difference: that between the assembled group and the lone victim; 'alone against all' is an inverted but equivalent version of the sacrificial 'all against one'.

Similarly, Adler's analogy replicates Girard's while it is turned around. The warrior sent abroad to die in glory like a sacred king and the warrior captured and brought home to be maintained in royal splendor till execution are the same figure viewed from opposite directions. The arena may appear different depending on whether one is seated with the home crowd or the visitors, but the game is the same. It is Verdier's 'regulated game' of vengeance,[30], Girard's 'agreement never to agree'.

The tacit complicity between opposing sides in this kind of vendetta is demonstrated by the fact, reported by Clastres, that an Indian captive well understood he could not go home again: 'among the Tupi-Guarani a prisoner of war could remain for years safe and sound, free even, in the village of the victors: but sooner or later, he was inevitably executed and eaten. He knew that and yet didn't try to flee', for were he to do so, 'the people of his village would refuse to take him in: he was a prisoner, his destiny must therefore be accomplished'.[31]

An arrangement to obtain victims by exchanging prisoners in battle achieves the same purpose as one which makes prisoners of internal transgressors. As Valeri observes, a 'defeated and fallen' Hawaiian noble 'can be considered "transgressed"',[32] and the 'transgressed' Tupi-Guarani warrior is expelled from his own group as surely as if he were a transgressor: 'the captured warrior no longer belongs to the tribe', Clastres emphasizes, 'he is *definitively excluded from the community* which' – paradoxically – 'is only waiting to learn of his death in order immediately to avenge him'.[33]

A member of the group must be killed so that the group may wreak vengeance; another group is needed to carry out the killing so that the vengeance will be directed outward. Ritualized vengeance becomes an aim in itself when it makes it possible to keep vengeance from spreading within the group. In this way the sacred duty to avenge highlighted by Verdier can be reconciled with the prohibition on vengeance stressed by Girard, for whom 'the interminable vengeance engulfing two rival tribes may be read as an obscure metaphor for vengeance that has been effectively shifted from the interior of the community'.[34]

To the modern observer, sacrifice proper looks much more like a religious ritual than does an endless vendetta. True, we are accustomed to seeing both sides in military struggles draw on religion for an extra fillip of pious justification, and we realize as well that some people genuinely fight to achieve religious ends opposed by their adversaries, but we have more difficulty in understanding how warfare could be a religious requirement in itself – especially warfare between groups which share the religious values of the larger society to which both belong. Yet wars were 'of' religion long before there were any 'wars of religion'. Religion provides the framework for forms of warfare which have nothing to do with struggles for power.

One of the purest examples of the displacement of internal violence on to external scapegoats in religious warfare is head-hunting. Renato Rosaldo, who lived with the Ilongots in the Philippines, calls their ritualized head-hunting 'very like sacrifice'. To take a head is a requirement of manhood. The young are led by older men whose prime motive for initiating an expedition is 'devastating personal loss. If . . . somebody close to them dies, they become enraged. . . . What these people say is that they need a place to carry their anger'.[35]

Rosaldo 'heard many reports of people learning of the death of somebody they've loved very much, being devastated by it, picking up a long knife, and just chopping up everything in sight', and he comments, 'When it's culturally available that one can go headhunting, that's the ultimate place to carry one's rage and anger. If it's not culturally available, then you hack up the furniture'.[36] In the absence of a culturally available external outlet, however, more than the furniture may be at risk – as Euripides reminds us in *Medea*. Girard quotes the lines spoken by the nurse, who vainly seeks to have the children kept out of Medea's sight: 'I am sure her anger will not subside until it has found a victim. Let us pray that the victim is at least one of our enemies!'[37]

Enemies are useful – so useful they sometimes must be invented, as any politician well knows. The modern state, with its monopoly of violence, renders unnecessary the prevention of internecine conflict through the violent unanimity of sacrifice. Nonetheless, a regime anxious to create consensus will still fall back on the unifying effect of internal or external threat. Even when the enemies designated are wholly secular, the language we use to describe the phenomenon betrays the religious origins of the technique: witch-hunting, demonizing opponents.

When the regime itself resorts to religious language to rouse the crowd against its opponents, we feel it is perverting religion by bending it to other ends – and so it is, in the case of a modern religion with a long history of separation of church and state behind it. The cynical exploitation of religion should not, however, lead us to believe that the religiously-couched designation of worthy victims is an invention of the state alien to the essence of religion. In fact, it is a unifying technique which is already part and parcel of religion in stateless societies like those analyzed by Clastres, where there can be no question of exploiting the technique to reinforce the power of the leaders because the latter do not exercise power as we know it. If anything, Clastres suggests, it is society in these groups which exercises power over the chief – the chief is the victim.

Like a social deviant, the chief or king is a marginal figure, often historically or mythically an outsider, who appears on the scene as an external threat which must be domesticated through the royal ritual, a process Marshall Sahlins describes in 'The Stranger-King'.[38] 'Kingship incorporates marginality as well as centrality', affirms Masao Yamaguchi, who notes, 'In the actual life of ancient Japan, princes were often executed for conspiracy and for incest'.[39] Incest is for Girard the typical example of a transgression 'that signifies the violent abolition of distinctions – the major cause of cultural disintegration'.[40] If cultural renewal and the reestablishment of differences are built on the sacrifice of a scapegoat blamed for provoking the dissolution of differences, it becomes clear why certain African kings destined for real or symbolic sacrifice are obliged to commit real or symbolic incest: 'The king must show himself "worthy" of his punishment'.

We saw that Girard likens the sacred monarch to the Tupinamba captive; indeed, he declares that the king 'reigns only by virtue of his future death; he is no more and no less than a victim awaiting sacrifice'.[41] Hocart believed that the wait was once very short. His comparative analysis of ceremonies from around the world led him to the conclusion that the original rite was at once a royal installation *and* a human sacrifice, implying that 'the first kings must have been dead kings' – a notion which only 'sounds absurd because we are accustomed to the idea of kings as directors of society. It sounds less absurd when we realize that the earliest kings did not govern'.[42]

In the case of kings who govern and retain a sacred character, it is sometimes found that the ritual pattern continues as a structural tendency even where actual sacrifice of the monarch is not institutionalized as part of the ceremonies. Sahlins explores the interface between myth and history in Fiji, where he correlates symbolic sacrifice in the rite of chieftainship with a historical trend noticed by one of Hocart's informants: 'Few high chiefs were not killed'.[43] According to Valeri, ancient Hawaiian succession regularly involves 'a violent confrontation among closely related pretenders. He who succeeds in sacrificing all the others becomes the only king', so that 'the kingdom is always *conquered* by its king, who, moreover, must constantly defend it from the "rebels", that is, from his rivals'. But, again, 'these rivals are not simply killed; they are sacrificed . . .'.[44] The succession struggle is 'real', the victory 'ritual', with the rivals or 'rebels' killed below the temple and their bodies offered up on the altars.[45]

Yamaguchi finds a similar conflation of ritual pattern and political history in Japan: 'The *Kojiki* chronicle tells us of the internal wars carried on between the fifth and seventh centuries, almost in a ritual way, every time a king died. Although *Kojiki* is a legendary record, it reminds us of the succession wars that were fought in the lacustrine kingdoms of East Africa, as well as of the ritual of rebellion of the Bantu kingdoms of southeast Africa . . .'.[46] Consideration of ritualistic succession battles in Africa prompts Girard to formulate the following remarks regarding the difficulty one can sometimes have in distinguishing ritual re-enactments and political events, a difficulty which we will later encounter in the case of Islamic succession struggles:

> . . . in a conflict whose course is no longer strictly regulated by a predetermined model, the ritualistic elements disintegrate into actual events and it becomes impossible to distinguish history from ritual. This confusion is in itself revealing. A rite retains its vitality only as long as it serves to channel political and social conflicts of unquestionable reality in a specific direction. On the other hand, it remains a rite only as long as it manages to restrict the conflictual modes of expression to rigorously determined forms.[47]

Let us return now to the segmentary society of the Muslim desert tribes and look at their feuding in this light. We suggested that the violence among groups as portrayed by Gellner could be understood as a ritual means of controlling violence through violence. The feud certainly channels real political and social conflicts, but in what way does the religious framework provided for the violence restrict it from getting out of hand? After all, as Gellner comments, 'observers are generally struck or appalled by the pervasiveness of violence', yet 'the system does not disintegrate into total chaos. How is this attained?'[48]

The answer Gellner proposes lies not so much in segmentary organization as such but rather in 'the religious style which it engenders or at least which it favours': 'The most characteristic religious institution of rural, tribal Islam is the living saint'. The saint enjoys a type of hereditary charisma, belonging to a lineage that typically invokes descent from the Prophet, and he fills a pacific role crucial to the smooth operation of the segmentary tribal system: 'At its many fissures it has a great need for arbitrators and mediators, and these can only function well if they are in it but not of it. Saintly status and, very often, obligatory pacifism, makes the mediators both viable and authoritative, standing as they do outside the web of alliance and feud. . .'.[49]

In his studies of the pre-colonial society of the Iqar'iyen, Moroccan Berbers of the eastern Rif, Raymond Jamous presents this mediation as the intervention of men of *baraka* or 'divine benediction' in the exchanges of violence among men of honor. Only a head of household protecting and exercising authority over a 'prohibited' domain, a domain of *haram*, can claim to be a man of honor. But the sense of honor is expressed most fully through violence and murder.[50] Indeed, participation in violence is required to maintain one's honor: 'Every man of honor knows that he risks death by wanting to engage in violence, but also that he must take this risk if he wishes to assert his value'.[51] An aggression also demonstrates that the object of attack is himself a man of honor worth challenging: 'Nobody would attack a musician or a Jew without dishonoring himself'. Honor is hence a value which rests on a 'paradox': 'it supposes the assertion of authority over the domains of "prohibition", and also the transgression of these prohibitions through challenge and counter-challenge'.[52] Thus, while Girard's theory would lead one to interpret the system of prohibitions as guaranteeing the differences that should constitute a bulwark against violence, the same system includes a built-in encouragement to violence.

This is where the men of *baraka*, the holy men or 'sherifs', enter the picture. As Jamous explains, 'The game of honor prevents the laymen from declaring their wish to interrupt the violence: that would be a demonstration of weakness. . . . Only the mediation of a man in whom non-violence is a virtue makes it possible to arrest – if only temporarily – the cycle of violence'. The success of a mediator's mission is what confirms his possession of *baraka*. As a tribute to his status, the victim's group consents to accept a payment in compensation for the murder instead of pursuing vengeance, which remains the more honorable course.[53] But the payment of blood money or the gift of a bride or servant in itself is not sufficient. The parties to the conflict must take part in a ritual of peace, a ritual centered on a sacrifice: the symbolic sacrifice of the murderer, displaced onto an animal victim.

The murderer's relations, accompanied by the sherif, bring the blood compensation and a sheep to the territory of his victim. They march in procession with the murderer at their head, 'hands tied behind his back and a knife between his teeth. He "offers himself in sacrifice"'. At the border of the victim's territory, a close relative 'removes the knife from the murderer's mouth and, instead of killing him, cuts loose his hands and cuts the throat of the sheep in his place'. The sherif then blesses the gathering, and everyone present shares in feasting on the meat of the sheep.[54]

The pivotal position of sacrifice in the transition from violent to peaceful relations can be understood as a logical corollary of Verdier's postulation that the 'sacrificial response to a crime within a community is the counterpart of the vindicatory reaction on the outside.'[55] Having the adversary parties share in a sacrificial rite indicates that they now form an association within which vengeance is forbidden, as it is within the group, where sacrifice takes its place. Sacrifice figures prominently in reconciliation ceremonies in many cultures. An example from the borderlands of the Islamized kingdoms of the central Sahel is particularly telling for what it reveals about the way in which sacrifice permits the participants to control violence by putting it into a form in which it can be externalized and hence expelled from the group.

Just as divine malediction will fall upon the party that breaks an Iqar'iyen pact of reconciliation,[56] the Moussey sought to assure peace by 'placing between the two enemy groups a magic barrier the trespassing of which would provoke the automatic punishment of the one responsible'. Note in passing the paradox that it is the creation of barriers, not their destruction, which brings harmony; this is consistent with what we said at the outset about religion's forging differences to keep people apart. Now, in one of the Moussey rites of peace, a slave – qualified to handle the dangerous power of sacrifice by virtue of his expendability – slices a live dog in two at the border dividing the two groups while intoning, 'Here *sulukna*, very powerful business, we slaughter an animal to you, that nobody may be killed any more!'.[57] And '*sulukna*', the name of the occult force invoked, means nothing other than vengeance.

In this example the identity of violence and the sacred is particularly transparent and the import of that identity more easily traced. We can see that the representation of the violent reciprocity of vengeance as something transcendent makes it possible to externalize it, to put it at a distance, and to begin to manipulate it for the social good. 'Successful sacrifice prevents violence from reverting to a state of immanence and reciprocity', writes Girard, 'that is, it reinforces the status of violence as an exterior influence, transcendent and beneficent'.[58]

In Girard's version of history, the evolution of religion is the story of a progressive transcendence of violence: first, in the sense of a projection of violence out of society and onto a transcendent divine; then, in the sense of a divine injunction to rise above all violence, to renounce pitting violence against violence whether through vengeance or through sacrifice. In *Le désenchantement du monde*, Marcel Gauchet views human history as the story of the progressive transcendence of religion: first, in the sense of a projection of the divine out of society; then, in the sense of society's leaving the divine behind. In Gauchet's reversal of the usual perspective, the rise of the 'great religions' corresponds to a 'decline' of religion as the ruling force of terrestrial existence, for the more absolute the monotheism, the less absolute the domination of the divine over human action. It is in pre-state societies that one finds the most thorough submission to a sacred law beyond human control, so that 'religion in its purest and most systematic form is at the point of departure, in that world before the State . . .'.[59]

'From this angle', Gauchet asserts, 'the emergence of the State appears clearly as the major event of human history'[60] because the domination of man over man, even if despotic, even if legitimized by religion, wrests the locus of power from the grip of the radically other and brings it for the first time within human compass: 'The power of a few in the name of the gods is the beginning – O how timid and dissimulated, but irreversible – of a power of all over the decrees of the gods . . .'.[61] The separation of Church and State is another decisive step on the road to liberation from the sacred: 'The more the apprehension of the beyond is strictly controlled by a specialized hierarchy . . . . the more the terrestrial sphere displays its own sufficiency, freeing itself from the omnipresent preoccupation of a supernatural that is better and better defined and contained. A gaping breach thus opens into which the temporal power will leap in order to plead the necessary independence of its task in the world and to claim, in the face of this spiritual monarchy, complete mastery of its own domain'.[62]

In attempting to reflect on the relationship between Islam and violence in the pages that remain, I take as my starting point the complementary perspectives afforded by the visions of these two contemporary thinkers: Girard's, in which religion progressively distances itself from an original unity of violence and the sacred, and Gauchet's, in which society progressively liberates itself from an original submission of the social to the sacred.

Girard has been dubbed the 'Hegel of Christianity',[63] and Gauchet, for whom Christianity promises to be 'the religion of the exit from religion',[64] could be aptly styled the 'Hegel of secular humanism'. Neither one includes Islam in his *welthistorischer*. Girard has not written on the subject, while Gauchet only refers to it a couple of times in passing, although he offers a clue as to how it departs from the grand design in his brief allusions to 'submission in belief'[65] and to the 'revelation supplied by the *Koran*, the very presence, irrefragable and literal, of the transcendent in the immanent'.[66] What about Georg Wilhelm Friedrich himself? Gellner recalls that Hegel had to 'indulge

in most painfully tortuous arguments in order to explain how an
earlier faith, Christianity, nevertheless is more final and absolute than
a chronologically later one, namely Islam'.[67]

My hunch is that Hegel's uneasiness holds the key to a theoretical
neglect of Islam that is far from being confined to Girard and Gauchet.
Fifteen years ago, sociologist Bryan Turner found the conscientious
sociologist of religion to be 'in the embarrassing position of facing a
massive gap in his knowledge of world religions':[68] 'In comparison with
the established and flourishing literature on other world religions and
their associated civilizations, the systematic study of Islam is a neglected
field in sociology, phenomenology and history of religions'.[69] The
problem, I suspect, is that Islam will not fit neatly into a preconceived
evolutionary scheme.

In particular, Islam does not conform to expectations raised by the
idea that it followed in the footsteps of the other 'religions of the book'.
The theorist proceeding on the basis of this idea will be disorientated
for a simple reason spelled out by Joseph Chelhod in a work that
Turner deems one of the 'major land-marks in Islamic scholarship,' *Les
Structures du Sacré chez les Arabes*:[70] 'the religious structures of Islam
are better understood when one compares them to the ancient Arab
cultural bedrock than when one seeks to illustrate them by borrowings,
often undeniable, from Judaism and Christianity'.[71]

Chelhod acknowledges that 'the incontestable influence of the ancient
Arab religion on Islam exerted itself essentially in the domain of beliefs,
rites and institutions; it hardly affected the intransigent monotheism of
Mohammad'.[72] Alongside this monotheism, however, 'it is immanence
which seems the dominant trait of the Islamic conception of the sacred,
as to behavior'. God as the ultimate controlling agency is superimposed
on an animist infrastructure; the divine transcends more manipulable
forms of the sacred which nonetheless persist – *haram*, *baraka* – so that
'one of the essential aspects of the sacred is to be intimately bound to
the profane activities of the believer'.[73]

Apparently, then, the terrestrial sphere is in Gauchet's terms still
characterized by an ubiquitous preoccupation with the supernatural.
Emmanuel Sivan reports the same finding after studying the religious
weeklies published by Egypt's ruling party and by the moderate Liberal
opposition: the world inhabited by the readers of these periodicals 'is
one where the natural and supernatural are inextricably interlaced.
A world populated by ghosts, the spirits of the dead, *jinn* (invisible
beings) of the harmful and of the helpful varieties; a world haunted by
the specter of the Tempting Satan and his demons, where the believer
may be succored by holy men and angels and, if need be, by miracles;

a world where communication with the dead (especially one's relatives) is an everyday occurrence, and where the presence of the supernatural is deemed quite real, almost palpable'.[74]

Religion and everyday activity are inevitably intermingled because the temporal power never carved out its own, secular domain. Indeed, 'the very notion of a secular jurisdiction and authority . . . is seen as an impiety', according to Bernard Lewis, who notes that until the nineteenth century the word 'secular' could not be translated into Arabic or Turkish, while even today these languages contain no equivalent terms for 'church' and 'laity'. For Muslims, Lewis emphasizes, religion is not a 'compartment of life reserved for certain matters, and separate, or at least separable, from other compartments of life'.[75] This is not merely the attitude of fundamentalists; it is also the diagnosis of a leftist critic:[76] 'Ours is a society which defines all its activities and the events occurring around it through ritual and relationship to God'.[77]

'Islam is the religion which has most completely confounded and intermixed the two powers', writes Tocqueville,[78] '. . . so that all the acts of civil and political life are regulated more or less by religious law'.[79] Rather than speaking of 'confusion,' it would be more exact to say that secular power never differentiated and detached itself from the religious matrix. Conversely, as Sivan notes, 'Muslim civil society (led or educated by the *ulama*), 'while disdaining the political sphere and harboring precious few illusions as to its evil nature, tends on the whole to acquiesce with the way its masters control it'.[80]

What does all this imply for the relationship between Islam and violence? If opposition to violence as such is not internal to Islam, that does not mean religion plays no role in the control of violence. Insofar as the lack of separation between religious and (what to us would be) other spheres of life is also characteristic of tribal religions, we might well expect to find in Islam the ritual procedures studied earlier for channeling violence outside the borders of the tribe.

But was it not the achievement of Muhammad to substitute a universal religion for a kinship-based tribal cult? It is no doubt true, as Turner observes, that 'the universalism of the new Islamic community (*umma*) based on faith rather than blood cut right across the particularism of the tribal system and its concomitant customs of blood feud and retaliation'.[81] However, it is also true that the Muslim community as a whole regards the universe beyond the Abode of Islam (*dar al-Islam*) much as a tribe would regard the world beyond its boundaries: it is the Abode of War (*dar al-Harb*).

It is a religious obligation to maintain a state of war with those outside the rule of Islam.[82] The standard Muslim greeting *salam 'alaykum*, 'peace be upon you', is reserved for addressing fellow Muslims and must not be employed in addressing non-Muslims – rather as if peace within the Muslim community were made possible only by forbidding peace with those on the outside.[83] In the same way, if the sherifs who are the peacemakers among the Iqar'iyen are the only men for whom non-violence is a virtue, it is not an absolute virtue even for them: the requirement for them to behave pacifically is lifted in the case of war against the infidel.[84]

This of course is the famous jihad or 'holy war'. The translation of the term is not beyond debate – literally meaning 'striving', it could be taken in a spiritual sense, and the tag 'holy' is redundant except as a reminder that all Islamic duties are ordained by God – but Lewis assures us that the 'overwhelming majority of classical theologians, jurists, and traditionists . . . understood the obligation of *jihad* in a military sense'.[85] More controversial, perhaps, is the use of 'jihad' for wars of aggression against unbelievers. Modern Muslim apologists have argued that jihad is in reality a purely defensive doctrine. It is worth noting the response that this approach elicited from the intellectual fathers of today's militant fundamentalism. According to Leonard Binder, both Abu'l-'Ala al-Mawdudi and Sayyid Qutb 'rejected this interpretation, finding in it an expression of false consciousness. Muslim apologists had been tricked into adopting an idea which not only conformed to the Christian religious doctrine, but one which also suited the political preferences of non-Muslim political leaders'.[86]

One might ask whether attributing to Islam a purely defensive military outlook would not in fact amount to an ethnocentric projection onto another religion of attitudes proper to the Western religious tradition. The ritual channeling of violence outward is a commonplace component of other religions – and is doubtless an equally common phenomenon in the West. The difference is simply that, as Gellner puts it, Christianity is 'ambivalent about its own bellicosity'.[87]

If, then, violence channeled outward against the infidels appears to be a ritual requirement in Islam, internal violence seems to accompany in ritual or quasi-ritual fashion the succession of a leader. Like the Hawaiian king, the sultan of traditional Morocco must conquer his throne and constantly defend it from rivals and rebels. The death of a sultan is regularly followed by a period of anarchy during which the pretenders fight it out to see which one has the superior *baraka*. The prosperity-producing sacrifice of the Hawaiian rivals or rebels by the victor also has its parallel in Morocco. As long as the future sultan hasn't vanquished his rivals and brought the rebels to submission', Jamous explains, 'his violence is the simple manifestation of his strength or weakness and places him on the same level as his enemies. But when his violence triumphs, it takes on another sense and becomes a sacrificial act in the course of which the hapless opponents of the new sovereign play the role of propitiatory victims offered for the reestablishment of the divine order and for the prosperity of the community of believers'. The violence that puts an end to the reciprocal play of violence against violence reveals its divine nature: 'The triumphant violence . . . is perceived as being of divine essence'.[88]

The *baraka* of the sultan only makes itself known retrospectively. Gellner sums up in like manner the way the *ulama*, or religious scholars, determine the legitimacy of Muslim rulers in general: 'the verdict of the *ulama* regarding legitimacy, like the flight of that much overrated bird the Owl of Minerva, takes place only after the event, and hence in effect ratifies the actual power situation, rather than sitting in judgment on it.'[89] Furthermore, while the Holy Law imposes limits on the power of the sovereign, Lewis notes a 'flaw': 'it established no apparatus and laid down no procedures for enforcing these limitations, and no device for preventing or challenging a violation of the law by the ruler, other than force'.[90]

But the overthrow of leaders by force seems to be built into the system. The survival rate of chiefs of tribal leagues among the Iqar'iyen is no better than that of high chiefs in Fiji. The chiefs of leagues in Jamous' historical survey were all exiled or killed by their own dependents,[91] as if they reigned by virtue of their status as sacrificial victims in waiting: 'Everything takes place in sum as if the Iqar'iyen chose men on whom they lavished praises before sacrificing them so to speak on the altar of honor, the supreme value perpetuated through offerings of the noblest victims'.[92]

The question I would ask in closing, then, is to what extent this model can be seen as paradigmatic of an Islamic political pattern rooted in the religion. A similar pattern seems to unfold at different levels with varying degrees of ritualization, beginning perhaps with the assassination of three of the first four caliphs to succeed the Prophet. In the absence of strictly determined forms, the sacrificial channeling of violence against violence is always in danger of spilling over into renewed revenge cycles of violence against violence, ultimately resulting in the confusion of ritual and history.

NOTES

1. René Girard, *Violence and the Sacred*, trans. by Patrick Gregory (Baltimore, MD and London: The Johns Hopkins University Press, 1977), p.146.

2. A. M. Hocart, *Kings and Councillors: An Essay in the Comparative Anatomy of Human Society* (Chicago, IL: University of Chicago Press, 1970 [orig. published in 1936]), p.40.
3. Lucien Scubla, *Logiques de la Réciprocité*. Cahier du CREA, No. 6 (Paris: École Polytechnique, 1985), p.76.
4. Girard, *Violence and the Sacred* (hereafter abbreviated as *VS*), pp.14–15.
5. Joseph Chelhod, 'Equilibre et parité dans la vengeance du sang chez les Bédouins de Jordanie' in Raymond Verdier, ed., *La vengeance*, vol. 1: *Vengeance et pouvoir dans quelques sociétés extra-occidentales* (Paris: Cujas, 1980), p.125; see also Joseph Chelhod, *Les Structures du Sacré chez les Arabes* (Paris: Maisonneuve et Larose, 1964), pp.151–2.
6. Chelhod, 'Equilibre et parité', p.130.
7. Girard, *VS*, p.15.
8. Raymond Verdier, 'Le système vindicatoire' in Verdier, ed., *La vengeance*, Vol 1 (Paris: Cujas, 1980), p.21.
9. Ibid., p.24.
10. Ernest Gellner, *Muslim Society* (Cambridge: Cambridge University Press, 1981), p.97.
11. Verdier, 'Le système vindicatoire', p.24.
12. Ibid., p.30.
13. Pierre Clastres, *Recherches d'anthropologie politique* (Paris: Seuil, 1980), p.206.
14. Alfred Adler, 'La guerre et l'Etat primitif' in Miguel Abensour, ed., *L'esprit des lois sauvages: Pierre Clastres ou une nouvelle anthropologie politique* (Paris: Seuil, 1987), pp.98–9.
15. Gellner, *Muslim Society*, pp.36–7.
16. Ibid., p.40.
17. Ibid., p.39.
18. Ibid., p.69.
19. Ibid., p.39.
20. Quoted in Verdier, 'Le système vindicatoire', p.39.
21. Valerio Valeri, *Kingship and Sacrifice: Ritual and Society in Ancient Hawaii*, trans. by Paula Wissing (Chicago, IL: University of Chicago Press, 1985), p.356.
22. Ibid., p.164.
23. Girard, *VS*, p.278.
24. Ibid., p.280.
25. Ibid., p.278.
26. Adler, 'La guerre et l'Etat primitif,' pp.111–12.
27. Clastres, *Recherches d'anthropologie politique*, p.232.
28. Ibid., p.237.
29. Ibid., p.234.
30. Verdier, 'Le système vindicatoire', p.30.
31. Clastres, *Recherches d'anthropologie politique*, p.236.
32. Valeri, *Kingship and Sacrifice*, p.374.
33. Clastres, *Recherches d'anthropologie politique*, p.236.
34. Girard, *VS*, p.279.
35. 'Discussion' with Renato Rosaldo in Robert G. Hamerton-Kelly (ed.), *Violent Origins: Ritual Killing and Cultural Formation*, (Stanford; CA: Stanford University Press, 1987), pp.242–3.
36. Ibid., p.252.
37. Girard, *VS*, p.9.
38. Marshall Sahlins, *Islands of History* (Chicago, IL: University of Chicago Press, 1985), pp.73–103.
39. Masao Yamaguchi, 'Kingship, Theatricality, and Marginal Reality in Japan' in Ravindra K. Jain, ed., *Text and Context: The Social Anthropology of Tradition* (Philadelphia, PA: Institute for the Study of Human Issues, 1977), p.165.
40. Girard, *VS*, p.98.

41. Ibid., p.107.
42. A. M. Hocart, *Social Origins* (London: Watts, 1954), p.77.
43. Sahlins, *Islands of History*, p.94.
44. Valeri, *Kingship and Sacrifice*, p.160.
45. Ibid., p.163.
46. Yamaguchi, 'Kingship, Theatricality, and Marginal Reality', p.165.
47. Girard, *VS*, pp.109–10.
48. Gellner, *Muslim Society*, p.40.
49. Ibid., pp.40–41.
50. Raymond Jamous, *Honneur et baraka: Les structures sociales traditionnelles dans le Rif* (Cambridge: Cambridge University Press, 1981), pp.67–9.
51. Cécile Barraud, Daniel de Coppet, André Itéanu and Raymond Jamous, 'Des relations et des morts: Quatre sociétés vues sous l'angle des échanges' in Jean-Claude Galey, ed., *Différences, valeurs, hiérarchie: Textes offerts à Louis Dumont* (Paris: Editions de l'École des Hautes Études en Sciences Sociales, 1984), p.493.
52. Jamous, *Honneur et baraka*, p.69.
53. Ibid., pp.210–12.
54. Ibid., p.212.
55. Verdier, 'Le système vindicatoire,' p.23.
56. Jamous, *Honneur et baraka*, p.212.
57. Igor de Garine, 'Les étrangers, la vengeance et les parents chez les Massa et les Moussey (Tchad et Cameroun)' in Raymond Verdier (ed.), *La vengeance*, Vol. 1 (Paris: Cujas, 1980), p.97.
58. Girard, *VS*, p.266.
59. Marcel Gauchet, *Le désenchantement du monde: Une histoire politique de la religion* (Paris: Gallimard, 1985), pp.x–xii.
60. Ibid., p.X.
61. Ibid., p.31.
62. Ibid., p.103.
63. Jean-Marie Domenach, *Enquête sur les idées contemporaines* (Paris: Seuil, 1981), p.107.
64. Gauchet, *Le désenchantement du monde*, p.ii.
65. Ibid., p.95.
66. Ibid., p.102.
67. Gellner, *Muslim Society*, p.7.
68. Bryan S. Turner, *Weber and Islam* (London: Routledge & Kegan Paul, 1974), p.2.
69. Ibid., p.7.
70. Ibid., p.2.
71. Joseph Chelhod, *Les Structures du Sacré chez les Arabes* (Paris: Maisonneuve et Larose, 1964), p.257.
72. Ibid., p.261.
73. Ibid., pp.255–6.
74. Emmanuel Sivan, *Radical Islam: Medieval Theology and Modern Politics* (New Haven, CT: Yale University Press, 1985), pp.135–6.
75. Bernard Lewis, *The Political Language of Islam* (Chicago, IL: University of Chicago Press, 1988), pp.2–3.
76. Nadim al-Bitar, 'Major Causes of Arab Political Physiognomy' in *QA*, May 1979.
77. Quoted in Sivan, *Radical Islam*, p.185.
78. Alexis de Tocqueville, *Oeuvres complètes*, vol 3.
79. Quoted in Gellner, *Muslim Society*, p.1.
80. Emmanuel Sivan, *Interpretations of Islam* (Princeton, NJ: The Darwin Press, 1985), p.109.
81. Turner, *Weber and Islam*, pp.35–6.
82. Lewis, *The Political Language of Islam*, p.73.
83. Ibid., pp.78–9.

84. Jamous, *Honneur et baraka*, p.193.
85. Lewis, *The Political Language of Islam*, p.72.
86. Leonard Binder, *Islamic Liberalism: A Critique of Development Ideologies* (Chicago, IL: University of Chicago Press, 1988), p.181.
87. Gellner, *Muslim Society*, p.42.
88. Jamous, *Honneur et baraka*, p.228.
89. Gellner, *Muslim Society*, p.115.
90. Lewis, *The Political Language of Islam*, p.113.
91. Jamous, *Honneur et baraka*, p.170.
92. Ibid., p.173.

REFERENCES

Adler, Alfred, 'La guerre et l'Etat primitif' in Miguel Abensour (ed.), *L'esprit des lois sauvages: Pierre Clastres ou une nouvelle anthropologie politique* (Paris: Seuil, 1987) pp.95–114.

Barraud, Cécile, Daniel de Coppet, André Itéanu, Raymond Jamous, 'Des relations et des morts: Quatre sociétés vues sous l'angle des échanges' in Jean-Claude Galey (ed.), *Différences valeurs hiérarchie: Textes offerts à Louis Dumont* (Paris: Editions de l'École des Hautes Études en Sciences Sociales, 1984), pp.421–520.

Binder, Leonard, *Islamic Liberalism: A Critique of Development Ideologies* (Chicago, IL: University of Chicago Press, 1988).

Chelhod, Joseph, *Les Structures du Sacré chez les Arabes* (Paris: Maisonneuve et Larose, 1964).

———— 'Equilibre et parité dans la vengeance du sang chez les Bédouins de Jordanie' in Raymond Verdier (ed.), *La vengeance. Études d'ethnologie, d'histoire et de philosophie*. Vol. 1. *Vengeance et pouvoir dans quelques sociétés extra-occidentales* (Paris: Cujas, 1980), pp.125–43.

Clastres, Pierre, *Recherches d'anthropologie politique* (Paris: Seuil, 1980).

De Garine, Igor, 'Les étrangers, la vengeance et les parents chez les Massa et les Moussey (Tchad et Cameroun)' in Verdier, ed., *La vengeance*, Vol. 1. (Paris, Cujas, 1980), pp.91–124.

Domenach, Jean-Marie, *Enquête sur les idées contemporaines* (Paris: Seuil, 1981).

Gauchet, Marcel, *Le désenchantement du monde: Une histoire politique de la religion* (Paris: Gallimard, 1985).

Gellner, Ernest, *Muslim Society* (Cambridge: Cambridge University Press, 1981).

Girard, René, *Violence and the Sacred*, trans. Patrick Gregory (Baltimore, MD: The Johns Hopkins University Press, 1977).

Hamerton-Kelly, Robert G. (ed.), *Violent Origins: Walter Burkert, René Girard, and Jonathan Z. Smith on Ritual Killing and Cultural Formation*, commentary by Renato Rosaldo (Stanford, CA: Stanford University Press, 1987).

Hocart, A.M., *Social Origins* (London: Watts, 1954).

————*Kings and Councillors: An Essay in the Comparative Anatomy of Human Society* (Chicago, IL: University of Chicago Press [first edition 1936], 1970).

Jamous, Raymond, *Honneur et baraka*: *Les structures sociales traditionnelles dans le Rif* (Cambridge: Cambridge University Press, 1981)

Lewis, Bernard, *The Political Language of Islam* (Chicago, IL: University of Chicago Press, 1988).

Sahlins, Marshall, *Islands of History* (Chicago, IL: University of Chicago Press, 1985).

Scubla, Lucien, *Logiques de la Réciprocité*. Cahier du CREA No. 6. (Paris: École Polytechnique, 1985).

Sivan, Emmanuel, *Interpretations of Islam* (Princeton, NJ: The Darwin Press, 1985).

——*Radical Islam*: *Medieval Theology and Modern Politics* (New Haven, CT: Yale University Press, 1985).

Turner, Bryan S., *Weber and Islam* (London: Routledge & Kegan Paul, 1974).

Valeri, Valerio, *Kingship and Sacrifice*: *Ritual and Society in Ancient Hawaii*, trans. Paula Wissing (Chicago, IL: University of Chicago Press, 1985).

Verdier, Raymond, 'Le système vindicatoire' in Verdier, ed., *La vengeance*, Vol. 1 (Paris: Cujas, 1980), pp.11–42.

Yamaguchi, Masao, 'Kingship, Theatricality, and Marginal Reality in Japan' in Ravindra K. Jain (ed.), *Text and Context*: *The Social Anthropology of Tradition* (Philadelphia, PA: Institute for the Study of Human Issues, 1977), pp.151–179.

Sacrifice and Fratricide in Shiite Lebanon

MARTIN KRAMER

Religion converges with violence at two points. The first is where religion is produced: by those who fashion and rework the beliefs and principles which congeal in a religious tradition. Such abstraction is a kind of intellectual production, and ultimately takes the form of accessible texts prepared by theologians and jurists. In the case of Islam, for example, the entire law of war is a series of codified abstract principles, defining when violence is obligatory, permissible, and forbidden, without reference to any particular situation. These principles have been compared, sometimes in useful ways, with other sets of abstract principles from other traditions.[1]

The second point of convergence is where violence is produced: by those inspired by religious vision to employ force. That vision may be quite remote from the principles codified by religious authorities, or it may closely reflect those principles. Yet ultimately it is here that violence takes its corporeal form, where hands take up blunt instruments, where people meet to plan harm and shed blood. This second convergence of violence and religion rarely occurs in the open. It is more likely to take place in a remote village, where an obscure cleric, an expert on explosives, and a young boy might interact to produce a startling deed.

This essay explores one such obscure point of convergence between religion and violence. In 1982 a Lebanese Shiite movement known as Hizbollah – the Party of God – mounted the first 'self-martyring' operation. A short time later, similar operations were organized by Hizbollah's Lebanese Shiite rival, the Amal movement. These operations took the following form: an individual would take the wheel of a truck or car loaded with high explosives, position that vehicle alongside a target, and detonate the explosives while still in the vehicle. In the resulting explosion, the driver was certain to die. The explosion also inflicted damage on the target, although its effect could not be predicted. The most destructive attack claimed 241 lives; other attacks claimed fewer casualties, and often only the life of the driver.

These operations were represented by those who claimed credit for them as straightforward acts of war. Hizbollah's attacks were directed against American, French, and Israeli targets in Lebanon; Amal's operations targeted Israeli forces in Lebanon. Yet from the outset, this classification posed problems. For while the operations were conceived largely as acts of war, and therefore as politically purposeful, their very structure suggested sacrificial rite. The perpetrators went deliberately to their deaths; the planners deliberately sent the perpetrators to their deaths. In this essay, I will suggest that these acts of self-sacrifice and sacrifice were not only designed for their maximum impact as acts of war. They also served the function which René Girard has suggested for sacrifice: the diversion and dissipation of violence born of inner feud.

Not only did these operations drive away the foreign enemies of Lebanon's Shiites; they also served to forestall the outbreak of fratricidal violence from within. The competitive cycle of sacrifice, done in the name of Islam, averted a competitive cycle of violence among adherents of Islam. When this sacrificial cycle collapsed, the violence turned inward upon Lebanon's Shiites, in the form of a fratricidal war. The point of this case study is not to deny the character of these operations as acts of war, but to suggest that they simultaneously served to maintain an internal equilibrium among those who initiated them. Girard posited the violence of sacrifice as the origin of all religion, as the escape from the vengeful spiral of feuding which will decimate a human community if it finds no outlet. In this case study, the purpose is to examine how a religious community maintains inner peace, by initiating an (obligatory) sacred war which fades at its edges into (forbidden) sacrificial rite.

It is necessary to begin with a caveat, which today must preface anything that remotely touches upon Islam. Violent acts committed by Lebanese Shiites – mostly by Hizbollah, but also occasionally by Amal – are the subject of fascination and fear in the collective consciousness of Muslims and non-Muslims. Such deeds occupy a prominent place in many polemical treatments of Islam. This is not completely unwarranted, because Islam does thoroughly permeate the self-representations of those who commit such violence. Their discourse, which serves to contextualize violence both for adherents and enemies, is laden with the evocative themes of Islam. Some of their leading figures are clerics in turban who parade in rallies with gun in hand, and who justify violent acts by reference to the sacred history and sacred law of Islam. There are Lebanese Shiites who believe, and insist that others believe, that everything they do, and every life they take, is in fulfilment of Islam's obligations. Yet the fact remains that Lebanese Shiism is a fragment of Islam, limited to a moment in the experience of Islam, and to a corner of the vast expanse of Islam. Nothing can be inferred about essential Islam from its experience.

The same can be said for the narrower context of Shiism. While Lebanese Shiism is a rather larger fragment of Shiism than it is of Islam, it is still only a besieged outpost of a faith within a faith. Hizbollah and Amal do employ the symbols of Shiism, and particularly the seventh-century martyrdom of the Imam Husain, since this resonates among Shiites of all classes. It particularly touches the poor, because the martyrdom is symbolically re-enacted once a year, and this often constitutes the most vivid and intimate experience of Lebanese Shiites with their tradition. Yet the proposition that these symbols predispose those who revere them to violence is untenable. Until recent times, few religious traditions so thoroughly disavowed violence as did the Shiite tradition long predominant in Lebanon as well as Iran.

For a thousand years Shiism in its predominant formulation was the creed of an oppressed minority, and deferred the obligation to wage jihad 'in the path of God' to the end of eschatological time.[2] Known for its passivity and quiescence in comparison with majority Sunni Islam, the Shiite tradition rested upon redemptive suffering, and most of its adherents did violence only to themselves in an annual penitential rite of self-flagellation. Historical circumstance transformed the unjust murder of the Imam Husain into a call for inner repentance rather than blood vengeance. Nor did the Shiite tradition urge martyrdom. The pursuit of martyrdom was deemed the heretical doctrine of extremist dissidents, not the duty of true believers. These were enjoined to survive and even disavow belief if faced with the prospect of persecution. This was nowhere in clearer evidence than in Lebanon. Until this century, Shiites dared not observe the anniversary of the Imam Husain's martyrdom through public processions and self-flagellation, as in Iran. Instead they met safely behind closed doors, where their grief took the form of mournful recitation of the tale of martyrdom. (The processions of self-flagellants, far from being an immemorial rite in Lebanon, are a twentieth-century innovation, first brought by Iranian immigrants.)[3]

The passage from weeping to self-flagellation was only the first step. The Lebanese Shiite community is in a process of stripping away these layers of pious restraint over violence accumulated through time and set down in books by earlier theologians. Parts of this community have revived the concept of sacred war between absolute truth and absolute falsehood. But neither Islam nor Shiism tell us why this generation of Shiites in Lebanon has reread tradition in new ways. They will not tell us why this community embraced a doctrine of sacred war that it had long ago disavowed, or why the obligation to survive has been displaced by the duty to sacrifice the self. The answers to these questions can only be provided by understanding the particular predicament of Lebanese Shiism. The first (and briefer) part of this essay is a preface, devoted to an interpretation of that predicament.

I

The Shiites of Lebanon are aggrieved. Lebanon is a multi-confessional society, composed of Maronite Christians, Greek Orthodox Christians, Sunni Muslims, Shiite Muslims, and Druze. For centuries these confessional communities enjoyed cultural and often political autonomy, assured by the forbidding topography of the country. But as western Europe established a globe-spanning hegemony, Lebanon was gradually integrated into the European-driven world economy, and absorbed the full impact of the West. This impact, however, was uneven, and the last to be touched were Lebanon's Shiites. Traditionally they were concentrated in southern Lebanon and the Bekaa Valley, two of the most remote regions of Lebanon. This afforded them some protection while they inhabited a corner of the Ottoman Empire. But once Lebanon had been constituted as a centralized and modernizing state, their isolation worked to their clear disadvantage. In their own areas, they suffered from the combined effects of neglect by the central government and exploitation by a semi-feudal landed elite of their own. Lebanon's Shiites rapidly fell behind Lebanon's other confessional communities by every quantifiable measure of social development, even as the dynamics of demography transformed them into Lebanon's largest single community. Eventually the surplus rural population began to flood into the least desirable parts of Beirut, where many lived in desperate conditions on a crumbling infrastructure built for perhaps a tenth of their number.[4]

Tied by their traditions to Iran, they had undergone an awakening in the 1970s under the guidance of Sayyid Musa al-Sadr, an Iranian-born cleric of Lebanese origin who fought neglect from without and exploitation from within. Sadr inspired a mass movement and militia known as Amal – an acronym, (meaning 'Hope') for 'Lebanese Resistance Battalions'.[5] This movement was reformist rather than revolutionary, and called for a reapportioning of Lebanon's resources to reflect Shiite demographic preponderance. Sadr disappeared in 1978 while on a visit to Libya, where he was probably abducted and killed for reasons unknown. But the movement did not disband, for by this time it had become the armed defender of the Shiite community in the civil war which had begun in 1975. Still, some of Lebanon's Shiites, caught between an escalating civil war in Lebanon and the loss of their leader, turned increasingly to Iran's triumphant revolution and its leader for inspiration and guidance. Iran, for ideological and strategic reasons of its own, encouraged Lebanon's Shiites to do so.

In the 1970s Lebanon's Shiites were made to assume another burden, as onerous as their despised standing in Lebanese society. Southern Lebanon abutted Israel, and increasingly became a battleground between Palestinian organizations and Israeli forces. Shiites responded either by fleeing the south, assisting the Palestinians, or resisting them. The level of violence in the south continued to escalate until 1982, when Israel invaded Lebanon to put an end to the Palestinian armed presence in the country. But although the Israeli invasion was not directed against the Shiites of Lebanon, it soon provoked their resentment. For Israel, despite its original intention, became an occupying power without a plan for withdrawal, and those who bore the brunt of this occupation were Lebanon's Shiites. Israel ultimately released its grip on Beirut, where the United States and France appeared as 'peace-keepers' in the very midst of the Shiite-populated quarters of Beirut. But Israel had no further plan for withdrawal, and many Lebanese Shiites discerned the outline of a plot to suppress the Shiites while Israel, the United States, and France fashioned their own order for Lebanon.

It is in this setting that Hizbollah first appeared in the summer of 1982. In the wake of the Israeli invasion, Iran sent a contingent of Revolutionary Guards to Lebanon, where they established bases in the Shiite-populated Bekaa Valley. They were joined by Lebanese Shiite dissidents from the Amal movement, and Shiites who had fought for Palestinian groups which had been driven from Lebanon. The new formation took the name of Hizbollah, the 'Party of God', after a verse in the *Quran* which promises victory to God's partisans. Pledging fealty to the Imam Khomeini, the movement declared its aims to be the transformation of Lebanese society into an Islamic order, the liberation of all oppressed Muslim peoples and occupied Muslim lands, and the transformation of a combined Islam into a world power on a global scale.[6] By the middle of 1983, Hizbollah had spread from the Bekaa Valley into the Shiite quarters of Beirut, where it mounted attacks, including 'self-martyring' operations, that eventually drove the Americans and French from Beirut. Shiite resistance to Israel soon followed, and took the form of a relentless guerrilla war. Both Hizbollah and Amal (as well as other leftist and pro-Syrian groups) contributed to the resistance, which took the form of ambushes, road-side bombs, and self-martyring operations.[7]

It was this war, and particularly the self-martyring operations, which captured the headlines. Yet beneath these events, which seemed to unite the Shiite community, a subtle process of fragmentation had begun. Before Hizbollah's appearance, virtually all of Lebanon's Shiites identified with Amal, subsuming their profound differences under the mantle of a charismatic leader. Hizbollah worked upon those differences, splitting families, neighborhoods, villages, and towns along existing lines, and infusing ideas into existing rivalries and feuds. Hizbollah raced through Lebanon like a hundred rivers along the dry beds of division that break the Shiite landscape of Lebanon. The potential for reciprocal violence was enhanced by the influx of arms, provided to Amal by Syria and to Hizbollah by Iran. On more and more occasions, in local settings, small-scale violence erupted, which took the form of gunfire and kidnapping between Amal and Hizbollah.

Yet for the first five years of Hizbollah's growth, that violence was contained and conflagration avoided. The clashes remained expressions of endemic local feuding, which sought shelter in the distinction between Amal and Hizbollah. But the much more consistent element in the relationship between the fraternal movements was imitative rivalry. They competed in professing their fealty to Khomeini, in distributing aid, in organizing marches, and in covering walls with posters. The violent dimension of this competition took not the form of internal strife, but competitive guerrilla war against the Western presence in Beirut and the Israeli presence in southern Lebanon. Both Hizbollah and Amal struggled to amass greater credibility as promoters of sacred struggle – in the number of attacks launched against foreign intruders, in the number of claimed enemy casualties, in the number of martyrs offered to the cause, and ultimately in the preparedness to mount self-martyring operations.

This struggle culminated in the withdrawal from Lebanon of the United States and France and the retreat of Israel to a narrow zone in southern Lebanon. To most observers, this represented an instance of successful and unified resistance against an onerous foreign occupation. Few noticed the evidence of imitative rivalry that drove the sacred war forward, and that channeled the growing antagonism between Hizbollah and Amal into competitive displays of violence against intruders. The competitive war served the vital function of absorbing the violence that would otherwise have manifested itself in conflict both between Amal and Hizbollah, and within those movements themselves. The jihad, while liberating the believers from foreign intruders, also postponed the incipient *fitna* – the destructive strife that threatened Lebanon's Shiite community from within.

II

The rivalry reached its apex in a series of self-martyring operations which were initiated by Hizbollah, and subsequently imitated by Amal.

No aspect of the struggle had the same effect upon the Shiite community
as these operations, which thrilled, fascinated, and repelled at once. This
was particularly true of the two operations, one by Hizbollah and one
by Amal, which first introduced the technique in the struggle against
Israel in southern Lebanon. The attacks against the US and French
contingents of the Multinational Force in Beirut were far more deadly,
but the anonymity of the bombers, preserved to this day, established a
distance between the community and the acts. But the poster visages
of the two self-martyrs who allegedly brought the method to the south
are readily recognized throughout Shiite Lebanon. So too is the lore
behind the visages. And within that lore are grains of evidence which
open new possibilities of interpretation. This is true even if the actual
identities of the self-martyrs cannot ever be independently established.
The following accounts, stripped of embellishment, convey the essential
information:

On 11 November 1982 a gas explosion gutted an eight-story building
used by the Israeli occupation forces in Tyre in southern Lebanon. In
the conflagration, 60 Israeli soldiers and 14 others died. The Israeli
authorities announced that the blast was the result of an explosion of
gas balloons, although there was considerable speculation that the attack
had been a deliberate bombing. Islamic Jihad did not claim the act as a
self-martyring operation, suggesting that it had been the result of time
bombs infiltrated into the building. Little more was said until May 1985,
when Hizbollah's Islamic Resistance gave a different account, claiming
that the building had been demolished by an explosive-laden car driven
by a self-martyr. The announcement attributed the act to Ahmad Qusayr,
a 15-year-old from Dayr Qanun al-Nahr, a Shiite town about ten miles
inland from Tyre.[8] It is impossible even now to pronounce definitively
on the origin or authorship of the explosion.

Ahmad Qusayr was born in 1967, and had an unexceptional childhood.
He left school after fifth grade and went to work for his father, who
ran a fruit and vegetable stall in the town. He then went to Saudi
Arabia where he worked for three months as a hospital orderly to
save money. Upon his return, he began to drive a pick-up truck
bought by his father, from which he sold produce. He would also
go regularly to the mosque for prayer, and help to decorate and
clean it. Like most local boys, he also enjoyed hunting and the
outdoors.

Ahmad did not become a fighter himself, but he fell under the
influence of young men who were fighters. He began to run small errands
for them, such as smuggling arms and tracking the movements of Israeli
patrols while he delivered produce. Then he began to drive the pick-up

to Beirut, leaving before sunrise and returning after sunset, without offering explanations. His father, who saw that he was not carrying produce on these trips, assumed he was running weapons. Then one day he borrowed his father's passport and transferred the registration of his truck to his father's name. He disappeared a few days before the operation, plunging his family into worry; his father went to Beirut to find him. Perhaps he had been kidnapped, perhaps he was being held by Christian militiamen. His parents learned of Ahmad's mission only when Hizbollah revealed his self-martyrdom two and a half years after the operation.

On 17 June 1984, a Lebanese car approached an Israeli military patrol in southern Lebanon. As the patrol and the car met, the driver of the car detonated high explosives packed in the vehicle, killing himself and wounding a number of Israeli soldiers. Credit for the operation was immediately claimed by Amal, which identified the self-martyr as Bilal Fahs, a 17-year-old from the town of Jibshit, near Nabatiyya in southern Lebanon.[9]

Bilal Fahs was born in 1967 to an impoverished family. His father sold vegetables from a cart, and lived in a one-room cinder-block house on the edge of town. Bilal's mother separated from his father a few months after Bilal's birth; the father remarried and had more children, crowding the house beyond endurance. Bilal spent most of his days in the room of his paternal grandmother. Bilal's father had not registered his marriage to Bilal's mother with the religious courts, which in Lebanon have jurisdiction over civil status. Bilal therefore did not receive an identity card, and so he could not be admitted to school, although he did learn to read and write. He drifted between Jibshit and the southern suburbs of Beirut, where he had aunts and uncles, and he did some occasional fighting for Amal. Eventually he became a bodyguard to Amal leader Nabih Birri. One year and two months before the operation, he became engaged, but encountered bureaucratic difficulties in legally marrying because his existence was nowhere registered and he had no proof of identity. The dynamic young prayer leader in Jibshit tried to help him straighten out the matter with the religious courts, but the outcome of this intervention is unknown.

Bilal's fiancée later said that during the three months before the operation, she saw a change in Bilal. He spoke at length about the prayer leader of Jibshit, allegedly killed at the hands of the Israelis, and listened to every item of news about the resistance in the south. He carried photographs of martyred fighters, read some Islamic books, and watched war movies and films about Islam. In his last letter, addressed to Amal leader Birri, he wrote: 'I will that my brothers in the movement all join hands in the jihad enjoined upon us by the Imam-Leader [Khomeini], and that we will persevere however many obstacles there might be, under the leadership of the giant fighter of the jihad, brother Nabih Birri'.

Like all evidence, this raises at least as many questions as it answers. Like all evidence, it is incomplete and perhaps it changes nothing. It is still possible to represent these self-martyring operations as a straightforward extension of war, and the product of the tactical acumen of their planners. Given the fundamental asymmetry of power between the two Shiite movements and their adversaries, the techniques of guerrilla warfare and self-martyring operations constituted a tactical response ideally suited to their limited resources. It is also possible to continue to represent them as acts of individual self-sacrifice, inspired by hatred of foreign intruders, religious vision, vengeance, or psychological disorder. Such interpretations have been suggested not only for these operations, but also for comparable instances at other times and places in Islamic history.[10]

But knowing the identities of the self-martyrs (or at least their alleged identities) while not banishing other interpretations, does suggest new possibilities. The one that emerges with the least coaxing is the existence of a social dimension of sacrifice in the operations. This dimension is still partly obscured from view, for the biographical accounts completely conceal the identities and methods of those who sponsored the self-martyrs. But the moment we become acquainted with Ahmad Qusayr and Bilal Fahs, we realize that while self-martyrs sacrificed themselves, they were also sacrificed by others. They were selected, prepared, and guided toward their self-martyrdom, a fact admitted in a general manner in the announcements published by sponsoring organizations after the operations. The self-martyring operations combined self-sacrifice and sacrifice, and blurred the distinction between the two. It is not at all certain that the two elements can now be separated for purposes of analysis. But the sacrificial dimension was most transparent in a simple truth about the operations: the self-martyrs were not self-selected, but had to meet criteria that were socially and culturally defined.

The precise criteria for selection were never made explicit, but the selected self-martyrs shared a number of characteristics that were valued above others. First, they had to be male. That this constituted a form of selection became evident in 1985, when a Syrian-backed nationalist party launched a wave of similar operations that included several women, among them Shiites. The laws of sacred war in Islam do not permit women to serve as combatants, and for Hizbollah or Amal to have employed women in these operations would have undermined their character as sacred acts of war. This position was explained by one of Hizbollah's clerics:

> One of the nationalist women asked me, does Islam permit a woman to join in military operations of the resistance to the occupation, and would she go to paradise if she were martyred? The jihad in Islam is forbidden to women except in self-defense and in the absence of menfolk. In the presence of men, the jihad is not permissible for women. My answer to this woman was that her jihad was impermissible regardless of motive or reason. She could not be considered a martyr were she killed, because the view of the law is clear. There can be no martyrdom except in the path of God. That means that every martyr will rise to paradise. I do not deny the value of the nationalist struggle *(nidal)* against Israel, but the jihad of women is impermissible in the presence of men. I do not deny women of the right to confront the enemy, but we must ask whether all of the nationalist men are gone so that only the women are left, or whether their men have become women and their women have become men.[11]

This position was confirmed after the self-martyrdom of Bilal Fahs, when his fiancée sought to 'join him in paradise' by undertaking an operation similar to his. Despite well-publicized efforts, she found no cleric prepared to declare her sacrifice permissible.

Second, the 'self-martyrs' had to be old enough to be deemed individually responsible for their acts, yet too young to have incurred the obligations of marriage. Their sacrifice could not be left open to the criticism that it had infringed upon the rights of parents or the claims of wives and children, from whom the planning of the act would have to be concealed. On the one hand, this meant that persons below a certain age could not be recruited. One of Hizbollah's clerics, asked whether young persons could fight without permission of parents, answered, 'When the plan establishes the necessity of their going out to fight, then going out is obligatory, and the agreement of the two parents is not necessary. If their going out is not necessary in the framework of the plan, then they must consult with the two parents'.[12] Since self-martyrdom did not demonstrably require a minor for operational purposes, and no parent would knowingly consent to a son taking part in such an operation, the employment of minors was virtually forbidden. But given the fact that death was assured in such operations, the same ban was extended to husbands and fathers. The sacred war of which the self-martyring operations were a part did include married men with families, some of whom were killed. But the fact of selection, by which the self-martyring operations passed into sacrificial acts, required more stringent limits. Given the early age of marriage in Lebanese Shiite society, this placed a low ceiling on the age of possible candidates. The remaining window of opportunity was correspondingly small. Ahmad Qusayr at 15 still lived at home, and was almost too dependent to qualify; Bilal Fahs at 17 was already engaged to be married, and almost too attached to qualify.

Third, the self-martyr could have no ties to anyone who might consider himself socially responsible for avenging the death against its sponsors, which would be conceivable were the operation to fail tactically. Ahmad Qusayr had no older brother, while Bilal Fahs was the sole product of a dissolved marriage without legal standing, and lived as an outcast. Girard writes that sacrificial victims must lack some crucial social link, so that 'they can be exposed to violence without fear of reprisal. Their death does not automatically entail an act of vengeance'.[13] The lack of fundamental social ties – to responsible parents, dependent wives and children, avenging brothers – rendered both of these self-martyrs acceptable candidates for sacrifice.

Finally, those selected for self-martyrdom had to have a minimal measure of pious intent, and no traits understood in surrounding society as signs of emotional disorder. 'The efficacy of the rites', writes Girard, 'depends on their being performed in the spirit of *pietas*, which marks all aspects of religious life'.[14] This spirit must embrace the self-martyr himself, and is usually demonstrated in a published will and the testimony of parents and friends. Motive must not be patently impure; if it is, the sacrifice is unworthy of the sacred cause.

Selection of the self-martyr, which is made secretly but on behalf of all, is thus a social and cultural selection. When the self-martyring operations are understood as collective rather than individual acts – as sacrificial acts – the dynamic of the sacrificial competition becomes clear. That competition took place on the level of sponsorship, as Hizbollah and Amal sought to demonstrate their capacity for mobilizing the many resources necessary for the operations. For Hizbollah and Amal were fraternal movements in an almost literal sense; lines of allegiance ran through families, villages, and neighborhoods. The pursuit of balance became fundamental to the preservation of peace between them, and when Hizbollah initiated self-martyring operations, Amal had no choice but to do the same. The sacrifice of Ahmad Qusayr (and the still unnamed self-martyr of Islamic Jihad who did a comparable operation a year later) sealed the fate of Bilal Fahs. If many of the foreign intruders also perished, so much the better, but the impure need not die with the pure for the act to be sanctified. Although Bilal Fahs killed no one it did not detract from the value of his sacrifice as a counter-point to the sacrifice of Ahmad Qusayr. The monument which Amal erected to Bilal served to commemorate the self-martyr and remind the community that his sponsors commanded the resolve and resources to sacrifice him for the good of all.[15]

That the military outcome of the self-martyring operations did not necessarily matter became apparent in their diminishing yield. Perhaps the first casualty of the competition was operational planning, which became less thorough as Hizbollah and Amal (soon joined by leftist and Syrian-sponsored parties) worked to outbid one another in the frequency of their operations. The sacrifice was no longer expected to obtain immediate results; self-martyrdom was presented increasingly as its own reward. At the same time, Hizbollah and Amal sought to elevate the standard of the sacrificial self-martyrs, by selecting slightly older youths who had more thorough religious and ideological commitment, and who had demonstrated the depth of their commitment by past involvement in conventional operations. One such instance was the bombing organized by Hizbollah on 19 August 1988, which sacrificed a most promising cadre, Haytham Subhi Dabbuq, from Tyre. Dabbuq was 20 years old at the time of his operation. He had joined Hizbollah's 'Islamic Resistance' at the age of 14, later taken part in conventional operations, and once had been wounded. After graduating from high school in 1986, he visited Iran, where he underwent religious and advanced military training.[16] From the point of view of selection, Dabbuq was the ideal self-martyr. From a military standpoint, it was considered unfortunate that his operation failed to kill any Israelis, but his death had its own redemptive quality and demonstrated Hizbollah's willingness to sacrifice its most promising young recruits. As purer self-martyrs were offered for fewer immediate results, the measure of sacred war in the operations diminished, and that of sacrifice increased.

III

So far, the role of the Shiite clerics has been omitted from this account, and for good reason. Their identities, like those of the actual planners and organizers of the attacks, are still unknown, making it impossible to define their role in the genesis of the attacks. It might have been the role of Lebanon's Shiite clerics, at some level, to have assured the self-martyr that his sacrifice enjoyed the highest sanction. According to one of Hizbollah's leading clerics,

. . . those who blew up the [US] Marines headquarters and the
Israeli military governate in Tyre [Ahmad Qusayr] did not martyr
themselves in accord with a decision by a political party or movement. They martyred themselves because the Imam Khomeini
permitted them to do so. They saw nothing before them but God,
and they defeated Israel and America for God. It was the Imam
of the Nation [Khomeini] who showed them this path and instilled
this spirit in them.[17]

But regardless of the role of the clerics in conveying this sanction to
the self-martyrs themselves, the support of the community depended
largely upon the verdict of clerics on the admissibility of the operations.
And since Hizbollah and Amal entered the sacrificial competition also
to win a larger share of Shiite allegiances, the sanction of the clerics
was valued by both. It was widely understood that the self-martyring
operations were religious acts, but only in an emotional sense. Religious
feeling had helped to generate them, but in a raw and dangerous form
with strong sacrificial overtones. They could be made *Islamic* only by
sanctification, which takes the form of reconciliation between the act
and abstract principle, done by those qualified to interpret sacred law.

The Shiite clerics had no difficulty in urging armed resistance to perceived enemies, and indeed did everything in their power to encourage it.
They achieved this, at least in part, by the transference of Shiite anguish
from self to other. That anguish found its most vivid ritual expression
on Ashura, the annual Shiite day of mourning for the seventh-century
martyrdom of the Imam Husain at Karbala. There were some whose
zeal for ritual self-flagellation on Ashura landed them in hospital,
especially in Nabatiyya in the south, where the practise had the longest
tradition in Lebanon.[18] Hizbollah's leading cleric sought to transform
such self-immolation into the immolation of others, when he called
upon self-flagellants to desist from the practice and join the resistance
against Israel:

Do you want to suffer with Husain? Then the setting is ready: the
Karbala of the South. You can be wounded and inflict wounds,
kill and be killed, and feel the spiritual joy that Husain lived
when he accepted the blood of his son, and the spiritual joy
of Husain when he accepted his own blood and wounds. The
believing resisters in the border zone are the true self-flagellants,
not the self-flagellants of Nabatiyya. Those who flog themselves
with swords, they are our fighting youth. Those who are detained
in [the Israeli detention camp in] al-Khiyam, arrested by Israel in
the region of Bint Jubayl, they are the ones who feel the suffering

of Husain and Zaynab. Those who suffer beatings on their chests and heads in a way that liberates, these are the ones who mark Ashura, in their prison cells.[19]

This kind of argument abolished a vital distinction, transforming struggle against the self – the ritual purpose of self-flagellation – into struggle against the other. And following the initial successes of the self-martyrdom operations, Shiite clerics were inclined to do the same, this time abolishing the distinction between death at the hands of others and death at one's own hands. According to Hizbollah's leading cleric, if the aim of one who destroyed himself in such an operation 'is to have a political impact on an enemy whom it is impossible to fight by conventional means, then his sacrifice can be part of a jihad. Such an undertaking differs little from that of a soldier who fights and knows that in the end he will be killed. The two situations lead to death; except that one fits in with the conventional procedures of war, and the other does not'.[20] In another formulation, he determined that 'the Muslims believe that you struggle with a gun by transforming yourself into a living bomb like you struggle with a gun in your hand. There is no difference between dying with a gun in your hand or exploding yourself'.[21] 'What is the difference between setting out for battle knowing you will die after killing ten [of the enemy], and setting out to the field to kill ten and knowing you will die while killing them?'[22]

Yet the ratio of ten to one could not be guaranteed, and when it dropped precipitously, the sacrificial dimension of the operations came into clearer focus. At that point, although operations continued to contribute to the inner equilibrium of the community, they had lost their value as acts of war. On that score, some Shiite clerics began to reason that the self-martyring operations had lost their Islamic justification. A failed military tactic now threatened to degenerate into a purely sacrificial rite. The Shiite clerics understood, as Girard writes, that 'the sacrificial act appears as both sinful and saintly, an illegal as well as a legitimate exercise of violence'.[23] And when it appeared more sinful than saintly, it had to be banned.

The Shiite clerics therefore issued a conditional ban. According to Hizbollah's leading cleric, 'we believe that self-martyring operations should only be carried out if they can bring about a political or military change in proportion to the passions that incite a person to make of his body an explosive bomb'. He deemed past operations against Israeli forces 'successful in that they significantly harmed the Israelis. But the present circumstances do not favor such operations anymore, and attacks that only inflict limited casualties (on the enemy) and destroy one building should not be encouraged, if the price is the death of the person who carries them out'.[24] 'The self-martyring operation is not permitted unless it can convulse the enemy. The believer cannot blow himself up unless the results will equal or exceed the [loss of the] soul of the believer. Self-martyring operations are not fatal accidents but legal obligations governed by rules, and the believers cannot transgress the rules of God.'[25] This ruling undermined the sacrificial cycle which had bound up Hizbollah and Amal in a competitive race to produce self-martyrs. A few more operations have been launched since then at very wide intervals of time. But the field was largely left to smaller factions, whose sponsorship of additional operations did not threaten either Hizbollah or Amal. Yet the end of the sacrificial cycle did not end the fraternal rivalry between Hizbollah and Amal. Its violence would soon find another outlet.

IV

One morning in January 1989 several Shiite villages in the area known as the 'Apple Region' of southern Lebanon became a killing ground. Before dawn a group of several hundred Hizbollah fighters, with photographs of Khomeini affixed to their chests, entered the villages by surprise. But this time their targets were not Israelis. Instead they sought out sleeping adherents of the rival Amal movement, and in the darkness a massacre ensued. Some of the victims were shot; others had their throats cut. In a few instances, the killing engulfed the families of the victims. This was later confirmed when photographers and cameramen entered the villages. One villager, choking back tears and standing over a pool of blood in his garden, told of how two masked men of Hizbollah had seized a member of Amal and slaughtered him 'like a sheep'. Clerics in Beirut had to issue rulings prohibiting the deliberate mutilation of bodies.

It was but one episode, albeit a particularly gruesome one, in the decline of Lebanon's Shiite community into *fitna* – internal strife, the antithesis of sacred war, pitting brother against brother in violence that threatens to destroy the community itself. For as Israel withdrew to a narrow belt in southern Lebanon, the fraternal movements of Hizbollah and Amal contested the ground they had liberated. The conflict that had always existed between Hizbollah and Amal now threatened to rise up and gut the Shiite community itself. 'Inevitably', writes Girard, 'the eroding of the sacrificial system seems to result in the emergence of reciprocal violence. Neighbors who had previously discharged their mutual aggressions on a third party, joining together in the sacrifice of an "outside" victim, now turn to sacrificing one another'.[26] The fratricide began in early 1988. Then came assassinations: one of Hizbollah's clerics was shot dead in an ambush done by Amal, two of Amal's foremost leaders in the south were gunned down in their car by Hizbollah. The weekly newspapers of both movements repeatedly published photographs of the bullet-torn bodies of the slain leaders.

The fratricide has continued ever since, punctuated by failed ceasefires mediated by outsiders. For sheer ferocity, these recurrent clashes matched any conflict between militias from different confessional communities. Clerics in the community appealed for an end to the conflict and banned the killing of Muslims by Muslims, but to no avail. For passions ran too deep, and the self-martyrdom operations had already made their destructive suggestion: that one Muslim might legitimately consign another to death in the name of Islam.

'Religion shelters us from violence just as violence seeks shelter in religion'.[27] The violence sheltered by Lebanese Shiism was perhaps that same violence which attended the birth of Shiism. It had been suppressed and subsumed, until all that remained was the sacrifice of tears, shed once a year for the martyrdom of the Imam Husain. But in our time, that violence has broken free of the bonds of pious restraint. Self-repentance yielded to self-flagellation, then to sacred war and individual self-martyrdom. With the passage to fratricide, some in Lebanon's Shiite community shed the last restraint. It remained to be seen whether the clerics could break the cycle by invoking the logical core of Islamic law, or whether the community would pass completely to the passionate pursuit of self-destruction.

NOTES

1. In particular, see Albrecht Noth, *Heiliger Krieg und Heiliger kampf in Islam und Christentum: Beiträge zur Vorgeschichte und Geschichte der Kreuzzüge* (Bonn: Ludwig Röhrscheid, 1966).
2. In theory, jihad can only be invoked in Shiite Islam at the command of the infallible Imam. Since that Imam is in occultation, the duty of jihad is theoretically in abeyance. However, there developed a contrary view that defensive jihad is permissible even in the absence of the infallible Imam. See Etan Kohlberg, 'The Development of the Imami Shi'i Doctrine of Jihad', *Zeitschrift der Deutschen Morgenländischen Gesellschaft* (Wiesbaden), Vol. 126 (1976), pp.64–86.
3. For the history of the rite in Lebanon, see Frédéric Maatouk, *La représentation de la mort de l'Imam Hussein à Nabatieh (Liban-Sud)* (Beirut: Centre de Recherches, Institut des Sciences Sociales, Université Libanaise, 1974), pp.41–48.
4. On the social transformation of the Shiite community, see Salim Nasr, 'La Transition des Chiites vers Beyrouth: mutations sociales et mobilisation communitaire à la veille de 1975', in CERMOC, *Mouvements communitaires et espaces urbains au Machreq* (Beyrouth: Editions du CERMOC, 1985), pp.87–116. The social place of Shiites among the other confessions in Lebanon is analyzed by Claude Dubar and Salim Nasr, *Les classes sociales au Liban* (Paris: Fondation nationale des sciences politiques, 1976).

5. On Sadr and the Amal movement, see Augustus Richard Norton, *Amal and the Shi'a: Struggle for the Soul of Lebanon* (Austin,TX: University of Texas Press, 1987) and Fouad Ajami, *The Vanished Imam: Musa al Sadr and the Shia of Lebanon* (Ithaca, NY: Cornell University Press, 1986).
6. On Hizbollah, see Shimon Shapira, 'The Origins of Hizbollah', *Jerusalem Quarterly*, No. 46 (Spring 1988), pp.115–30; and Martin Kramer, 'The Moral Logic of Hizbollah', in Walter Reich, ed., *Origins of Terrorism: Psychologies, Ideologies, Theologies, States of Mind* (Cambridge: Cambridge University Press, 1990), pp.131–57.
7. A comprehensive narrative of Lebanese Shiite affairs, with an emphasis on this post-1982 period, is provided by Andreas Rieck, *Die Schiiten und der Kampf um den Libanon. Politische Chronik 1958–1988* (*Mitteilungen des Deutschen Orient-Instituts*, 33) (Hamburg: Deutsches Orient-Institut, 1989). For the social and military dynamics of the resistance against Israel, see Elisabeth Picard, 'De la communauté-classe à la Résistance Nationale. Pour une analyse du rôle des Chi'ites dans le système politique libanais (1970–1985)', *Revue française de science politique* (Paris), Vol. 35, No. 6 (Dec. 1985), pp.999–1027; and W. A. Terrill, 'Low Intensity Conflict in Southern Lebanon: Lessons and Dynamics of the Israeli-Shi'ite War', *Conflict Quarterly* (Fredrickton, New Brunswick), Vol. 7, No. 3 (1987), pp.22–35.
8. Ahmad Qusayr's identity was first revealed in Hizbollah's weekly newspaper, *al-Ahd* (Beirut), No. 48, 24 May 1985. The biographical information is drawn on the obituaries reproduced in *al-Amaliyyat al-istishhadiyya: Watha'iq wa-suwar* [The Self-Martyring Operations: Documents and Photographs] (Damascus, 1985), pp.22–35.
9. Details on Fahs and photographs, *al-Amaliyyat al-istishhadiyya*, pp.68–81.
10. See Stephen Frederic Dale, 'Religious Suicide in Islamic Asia: Anticolonial Terrorism in India, Indonesia, and the Philippines', *Journal of Conflict Resolution* (Beverly Hills, CA), Vol. 32, No. 1 (March 1988), pp.37–59. While Dale interprets these instances in the narrow context of resistance to imperialism, his article suggests that the materials preserved in the records of past colonial governments are rich enough to allow an analysis at other levels, including the sacrificial.
11. Interview with Shaykh Abd al-Karim Ubayd, *al-Safir* (Beirut), 28 July 1986. This is the Shiite cleric who gained international renown following his abduction by Israel in July 1989.
12. Al-Sayyid Muhammad Husayn Fadlallah, *al-Muqawama al-Islamiyya: Afaq wa-tatallu' at* (Beirut: Lajnat Masjid al-Imam al-Rida, 1985, p.118.
13. René Girard, *Violence and the Sacred*, trans. by Patrick Gregory, (Baltimore MD and London: The Johns Hopkins University Press, 1977), pp.12–13.
14. Ibid., p.20.
15. A photograph of this monument appears in the Lebanese weekly *Nouveau Magazine*, 17 June, 1989, p.60.
16. Dabbuq's obituary in *al-Ahd*, No. 220, 9 Sept. 1988.
17. Speech by Sayyid Ibrahim al-Amin, *al-Ahd*, No. 135, 23 Jan. 1987.
18. For an account of the recent development of this rite, see Yves Gonzales-Quijano, 'Les interprétations d'un rite: célébrations de la "Achoura au Liban', *Maghreb-Machrek* (Paris), No. 115 (Jan.-Feb.-March 1987), pp.5–28.
19. Speech by Fadlallah, *al-Nahar* (Beirut), 27 Sept. 1985.
20. Interview with Fadlallah, *Politique internationale* (Paris), No. 29 (Autumn 1985), p.268.
21. Interview with Fadlallah, *Middle East Insight* (Washington, DC), Vol. 4, No. 2 (June/July 1985), pp.10–11.
22. Al-Sayyid Muhammad Husayn Fadlallah, *al-Muqawama al-Islamiyya fi al-Janub wal-Biqa al-Gharbi wa-Rashayya: tatallu'at wa-afaq; Nass al-muhadara allati alqaha samahat al-allama al-mujahid al-Sayyid Muhammad Husayn Fadlallah fi kulliyat*

idarat al-a 'mal wal-iqtisad al-far al-awwal, bi-ta'rikh 19 Shawwal 1404 al-muwafiq 18 Tammuz 1984 (n.p., n.d.), p.18.
23. Girard, *Violence and the Sacred*, p.20.
24. Interview with Fadlallah, *Monday Morning* (Beirut), 16 Dec. 1985. Fadlallah specifically mentioned the operation undertaken by Ahmad Qusayr in Tyre, as well as a later operation near Metulla, as 'successful'.
25. Speech by Fadlallah, *al-Nahar*, 14 May 1985.
26. Girard, *Violence and the Sacred*, p.40.
27. Ibid., p.24.

Violence and Catastrophe in the Theology of Rabbi Meir Kahane: The Ideologization of Mimetic Desire

EHUD SPRINZAK

In 1976, following a brutal terrorist attack on a school in the Israeli border town of Kiriyat Shmone, an attack that took the lives of many children, the late Rabbi Meir Kahane, leader of the extremist movement Kach (Thus!) wrote a short essay, *hillul hashem* (the desecration of the name of God). In the essay, which was never published and was only available for Kach members in a mimeograph form, Kahane presented his answer to the Kookist theology of Gush Emunim (the Block of the Faithful) regarding the process of heavenly redemption and the origins of the State of Israel. It was also the first time that he fully developed his revenge theory and elaborated upon the kind of violence he has been engaged in since 1969.

> The debate about the religious legitimacy of the State of Israel and its place in our history has already been conducted within religious circles for a long time. It has focused on the penetrating and real question: How can a religious Jew see the hand of God in a state that was established by Jews who not only do not follow the paths of God, but reject Him openly or, at best, are passive to His blessed existence? . . .
>
> The State of Israel was established not because the Jew deserved it, for the Jew is as he has been before, rejecting God, deviating from his paths and ignoring His Torah, but all this is immaterial to the case. God created this state not for the Jew and not as a reward for his justice and good deeds. It is because He, be blessed, decided that He could no longer take the desecration of his name and the laughter, the disgrace and the persecution of the people that was named after him, so He ordered the State of Israel to be, which is a total contradiction to the Diaspora.
>
> If the Diaspora, with its humiliations, defeats, persecutions, second class status of a minority . . . means hillul hashem, then a sovereign Jewish State which provides the Jew home, majority status, land of his own, a military of his own and a victory over

the defeated Gentile in the battlefield – *is exactly the opposite*, Kidush Hashem (the sanctification of the name of God). It is the reassertion, the proof, the testimony for the existence of God and his government.[1]

Kahane's short essay was a major attack on the prevailing Zionist ideo-theology of the time, the Kookist philosophy of Gush Emunim. According to Rav Kook Sr., the founder of the Kookist school, the State of Israel was created by the Zionists as part of a heavenly plan to redeem the people of Israel. The founding fathers of Zionism who established the secular movement in a clear defiance of most orthodox authorities were not sinful heretics who acted against God and abrogated his orders. Although secular and unobserving they were, unknowingly, God's holy emissaries. God Himself acted to revive the nation and in His mysterious way chose to do it through the secular Zionists. The secular State of Israel, according to the Kookist school is therefore not a sin but a reward, a graceful indication that God has finally decided to forgive *all* his people, not just the orthodox faithful. It is holy for its intrinsic value, for what it is and does for the Jews.[2]

In total contrast to Gush Emunim, Rabbi Meir Kahane believed that 'not the Jews, are responsible for the establishment of the State of Israel but, paradoxically, the Gentiles'. The State of Israel was established not because the Zionists, 'who did not repent(!)', deserved it, but as a result of the actions of the Gentiles. The perennial humiliation of the Jew by the Gentile world was, according to this strange theory, also a humiliation of God since his chosen people were being repeatedly persecuted. Following the Holocaust, God could no longer stand this humiliation and had the State of Israel established as his revenge against the Gentiles. Thus, the Jewish State is virtuous not because of what it does to the Jews but for what it inflicts upon the Gentiles. It is not an expression of reward but of punishment. Not the Jews deserve it but the Gentiles![3] The specific Gentile may not be the same, but he is always there, the Nazis, the Blacks, the Christian Church, the Russians, and, of course, the Arabs.

Kahane's intense radicalism, immense passion, and irrevocable commitment to his political struggle seemed to be exclusively rooted in this one element, the insatiable urge to beat the *Goy* (Gentile), to respond in kind for the two-milleniums old vilification of the Jews. Many Jews have expressed since time immemorial the Jewish antagonism towards the cruel Gentile nations which have repeatedly harassed and persecuted them and were responsible for their mass murder. A review of Kahane's writings leaves no doubt that he was by far the most extreme

representative of this school in modern times. Kahane's hostility to the
Gentiles may not be the cardinal presupposition of his political theology,
but it is certainly its most dominant emotional and psychological theme.
And what was unique about Kahane was that he openly sought revenge.
So strong was the rabbi's rejection of the Gentile world and his urge for
revenge that it may not be erroneous to sum up the Kahane assertive
psychology by the phrase 'I take revenge therefore I am'. And since the
rabbi believed he expressed the opinion of the Halakha (Jewish Law)
and the voice of God, it is not surprising that the vengeance the Jews
are expected to take is according to him not simply a personal act, but
God's very revenge for the humiliation He Himself suffered through the
desecration of his people.

> Do you want to know how the Name of God is desecrated in the
> eyes of the mocking and sneering nations? It is when the *Jew*, His
> people, His chosen, is desecrated! When the *Jew* is beaten, God is
> profaned! When the *Jew* is humiliated God is shamed! When the
> *Jew* is attacked it is an assault upon the Name of God! . . .
> Every pogrom is a desecration of the Name. Every Auschwitz
> and expulsion and murder and rape of a Jew is the humiliation of
> God. Every time a Jew is beaten by a Gentile because he is a Jew,
> this is the essence of hillul hashem! . . .
> An end to Exile – that is Kidush Hashem (the sanctification
> of the name of God). An end to the shame and beatings and
> the monuments to our murdered and our martyrized. An end to
> Kaddish and prayers for the dead . . . An end to the Gentile fist
> upon a Jewish face. . . .
> A Jewish fist in the face of an astonished Gentile world that
> had not seen it for two millennia, this is Kidush Hashem. Jewish
> dominion over the Christian holy places while the Church that
> sucked our blood vomits its rage and frustration. This is Kidush
> Hashem. A Jewish Air Force that is better than any other and that
> forces a Lebanese airliner down so that we can imprison murderers
> of Jews rather than having to repeat the centuries old pattern of
> begging the Gentile to do it for us. This is Kidush Hashem . . .
> Reading angry editorials about Jewish 'aggression' and 'violations'
> rather than flowery eulogies over dead Jewish victims. That is
> Kidush Hashem.[4]

Kahane's use of the formal Halakhic terminology of hillul hashem
(the desecration of the name of God), and kiddush hashem (the
sanctification of the name of God), should not mislead the reader to
believe that this is a conventional Jewish discourse. What really comes

out of these emotional statements is Kahane's idiosyncratic conviction that the very definition of Jewish freedom implies the ability to humiliate the Gentile. The stronger the Jew is, the more violent and aggressive, the freer he becomes. Kahane may not have gone as far as George Sorel and Franz Fanon in claiming that violence is a moral force in history or that violence sets one free, but he shared many similarities with both, especially Fanon.[5] For in a sense he proposed that Jewish independence and a Jewish State are not enough. Jewish sovereignty does not provide a full and satisfactory solution for the Jewish problem, for it only solves the misery of exile.

There is, however, another wound which has to be healed, the pain of humiliation, the misery of thousands of years of discrimination and victimization, the bleeding memories of generations of vilified Jews, killed for their religion. Kahane, it is important to stress, did not concentrate solely on the Holocaust, though his profound reaction to the Nazi genocide of the Jews during World War II had been a dominant theme in his actions and writings since the days of the American Jewish Defence League (JDL): The Holocaust was a natural product of anti-Semitism which could develop in any 'normal' nation and is still a historical possibility.[6] According to Kahane, the Holocaust, and the countless pogroms that preceded it, left in the nation's collective psyche an almost irreparable damage. Jewish independence alone cannot redress the damage, only a concrete revenge, a physical humiliation of the Gentiles. Therefore, Kahane, just as Franz Fanon, was not satisfied with a peaceful liberation. A military force that astonishes the world is needed, 'a fist in the face of the Gentile'.[7]

Catastrophic Messianism

An examination of the style of Kahane's writings and public speeches reveals that his revenge theory and legitimation of Jewish violence are consistently intermingled with a sense of disaster and tragedy. Jewish history since the destruction of the Second Temple is according to him nothing but a series of horrendous holocausts, the last of which has finally moved God to establish the State of Israel and avenge His desecrated honor. It is therefore not surprising that the other side of Kahane's 'logical' theology of violence was his emotional sense of catastrophe, a deep conviction that before the Jewish condition will get better things will become a much worse. Long before the evolution of Kahane's pessimistic prophesies regarding the future of the present State of Israel he made himself the prophet of doom and gloom of American Jewry. An essential part of his personal decision to move to Israel was his growing 'catastrophic Zionism', a fully-fledged ideology which predicted the inevitable coming of a new holocaust and called upon the Jews of Diaspora to move to Israel before it became too late. Nineteenth-century Zionism, it should be recalled, had a very strong catastrophic component. Its most influential theoreticians, Leo Pinsker and Theodor Herzl, came to their conclusion that Zionism was inevitable as result of the physical insecurity of the Jews in eastern Europe at the turn of the century. They convinced themselves as well as many generations of young Zionists that the anti-Semitism of their time was so severe that it was just a matter of time before the entire nation was eliminated by either physical destruction or spiritual assimilation.[8] The doctrine of *Shlilat Hagalut* (the Negation of Diaspora) was a direct product of this catastrophic Zionism.

Catastrophic Zionism started to decline following the evolution of the Zionist enterprise in Palestine and the success of the post-1917 political Zionism. With the exception of Vladimir Jabotinsky's 1930s warnings of growing European anti-Semitism it greatly declined. The 1948 establishment of the State of Israel, the emergence of the powerful American Jewry and the respectable presence of Jewish communities all over the democratic West have left the thesis of catastrophic Zionism with little explanatory power. But Kahane did not care less. In 1968 he began to talk about the gathering storm and the incipient disaster. It was just a question time before the enemies of the Jews overcame their guilt feelings about the destruction of European Jewry and started to plan the new holocaust. America of the melting pot, the dream country of millions of Jewish immigrants, Kahane told his audience, had started to undergo in the 1960s an economic recession, as well as severe moral and social crisis. It was just a question of time before the classical scapegoat, the Jew, was discovered and acted upon.[9]

Kahane's 'catastrophic Zionism' was the rationale behind his 'program for Jewish survival', the subtitle of his 1972 book *Never Again* and his comprehensive call for a series of steps in order to save American Jewry from extinction. While most of the suggestions had to do with an internal reform of Jewish life in America, the ultimate step called for was immigration to Israel. As much as Jews could help themselves in Diaspora by returning to full Judaism and by defending their rights and dignity, the Diaspora was doomed. The deterministic logic of anti-Semitism which was rediscovered by the vociferous rabbi left no chance for a long range Jewish survival outside of the State of Israel.[10] And while America of the 1960s was portrayed by Kahane as a troubled land, a modern version of Sodom and Gomorrah, Israel, the modern reincarnation of the land of the prophets and great conquerors was all good. It was the true answer to all the Jewish miseries of the time. The young state which managed to free itself by force from British colonialism and to build a military machine capable of defeating all the Arab anti-Semites was the manifestation of all of Kahane's early dreams. It had provided the only conditions for the breeding of the new Jew, a healthy and complete Hebrew national.[11]

Kahane's 1971 immigration to Israel and his increasing disappointment with its secular culture (and with the refusal of its leaders to listen to him) had made him reformulate his catastrophic theory. In 1973 and 1974 the leader of the JDL wrote two long essays: *Israel's Eternity and Victory* and *Numbers 23:9*, in which he first developed his catastrophic Messianism.[12] The entire theory was based on a verse from Isaiah 'In its time, I will hurry it (the redemption)' (Isaiah 60), and on its Rabbinical interpretation 'If they, the Jews, merit it I will hurry it. If they do not merit it, it will come "in its time"' (Sanhedrin 93). Redemption, according to this theory, is inevitable. It is part of God's plan and does not depend on what the people of Israel do or do not do. What is, however, left to the Jews is *the choice*, the determination of how and when does redemption take place. If they repent then, according to Kahane's interpretation of the sources, 'I will hurry it' meaning that redemption will come quickly and without pain. But if they do not, then redemption will come 'in its time', that is, following great troubles, wars and immense disasters. The establishment of the State of Israel in 1948 and 1967 victory of the Six Day War were unmistakable signs for God's desire to 'hurry it' provided the right attitude of the nation and its readiness to repent. Following the ordeal of the Yom Kippur War (1973), which indicated the existence of a serious problem on the road to salvation, Kahane saw fit to warn the people of Israel about the awaiting disasters should they not respond to God's gesture and return to orthodox Judaism.

In 1980 Kahane had plenty of time to reconsider his grand ideo-theology. He was placed on 'administrative arrest' of nine months in the Ramla maximum security prison for planning to blow up the Muslim Dome of the Rock on the Temple Mount. The months were one of his most productive periods, for he completed two major books, *Thorns in Your Eyes* and *On Redemption and Faith*. However, the most original essay he wrote in jail was *Forty Years*. The book's novelty was Kahane's daring conclusion that in 1948, the year Israel obtained its independence, the nation was given a grace period of forty years in order to repent and to prepare for God's hurried redemption. But there was an implied warning in the deal. If no repentance took place, an inevitable redemption ('in its time') was to occur, not out of God's grace but out

of His fury and through a tremendous disaster. The miraculous victory
in 1967 indicated that God had been keeping His promise and that it
was now time for the people to fulfill its part. But by 1980, just eight
years before the final deadline, no repentance had yet taken place and
the nation's time was running out.

> Consider, Jew. If it is indeed true what I say, then the refusal to
> heed is more than mere luxury. It is destruction. And then consider
> a second thing. *If it is true that the forty years began with the rise of
> the State – how many years are left?*
> Too few. So little time to make the great decision that will either
> bring us the great and glorious redemption, swiftly, majestically,
> spared the terrible sufferings and needless agonies, or G-d forbid,
> the madness of choosing the path of unnecessary, needless holo-
> caust, more horrible than anything we have yet endured. As we
> stand on the crossroads, with one direction that of glorious life and
> redemption, and the other the path of prior tragedy and holocaust,
> the choice is ours. We are the masters of our destiny if we will only
> choose the path that the Al-Mighty pleads us to walk upon.
> My people; my dear and foolish people! We speak of your life
> and those of your seed, your children and grand children. Choose
> wisely! The Magnificence is yours for the asking. The horror will
> be yours for the blindness. Choose life, but quickly; there is little
> time left. *The forty years tick away.*[13]

From 1980 Kahane became Israel's prophet of doom and gloom. Apart
from his political programs that called for the expulsion of the Arabs
from Israel and for the Judaization of the country, his books were full
of warnings regarding the coming catastrophe. It is very hard to tell how
deeply the leader of Kach believed in his own predictions, and whether
we had here an article of faith of a prophet in the tradition of Jeremiah,
or an expression of a troubled person who knew no one took his theories
seriously. But Kahane did discuss the issue of catastrophe in private
interviews, and said that even if he was the prime minister a catastrophe
would still take place if the nation did not repent willingly.[14]

Creating a Violent Order

One of the most characteristic elements of Kahane's career was that
unlike many high priests of violence and catastrophe, his teachings never
remained in the books. In fact, many of Kahane's theories, had been
written *after the fact*, after the JDL's or Kach's violent operations had
already been conducted. Had the extremist rabbi been entrusted with

power he might just as well have created the catastrophe he had been warning against all along. Thus an essential part of the Kahane phenomenon is the conscious attempt on his behalf to create a violent order, to shape a Kahane-inspired *weltanschauung* in which anti-Gentile violence and terror are part of the rules of the game. Already in the days of the American JDL, Kahane emphasized the importance of physical force. One of the pillars of the JDL's operative ideology was the notion of 'Jewish iron'. Kahane, it is true, did not invent either the idea or the metaphor: he adopted it from the ideology of Vladimir Jabotinsky, the ideologue of Revisionist Zionism. The expression *Barzel Yisrael* (Iron Israel), according to Jabotinsky, meant that in the Diaspora or under foreign rule, Jews were no longer to bow to their oppressors but were called upon respond to them in kind and with physical force, if necessary. It also meant that the sovereign Jewish State should have a strong army, capable of defending it against all threats. Kahane was so impressed with the notion of 'iron' and the application of physical force for self-defense, that he divided the JDL in America into two groups: the *Chaya* groups and the Scholar groups. Chaya in Hebrew means animal, and Chaya squads were in charge of the use of violence against the League's rivals.[15] Teaching his young followers to act and feel like animals, Kahane wanted them to believe that the JDL was the core group of a new breed, free of the traditional Jewish 'ghetto mentality'. and that they themselves were like 'the Jews of old'.

> Once upon a time, the Jew was not a member of the ADL [the American liberal Anti-Defamation League, an organization highly critical of the JDL's violence] – neither in form nor in spirit. It was not in the role of Mahatma Gandhi that the Jews fought at Massada; the men of Bar-Kochba and Judah Macabee never went to a Quaker meeting. The Jews of old – when Jews were knowledgeable about their religion, when they turned the page of the Jewish Bible instead of turning the Christian cheek – understood the concept of the Book and the Sword. It was only in the horror of the ghetto with its fears, neuroses, and insecurities that the Jew began to react in fright rather than with self-respect. That is what the ghetto does to a Jew.[16]

When he was brought to trial in New York in 1971, one of the main charges against Kahane was illegal possession of guns, ammunition and explosives. The leader of the JDL, who did not hesitate to ally himself with the Mafia boss Joseph Colombo – who established in New York the fake Italian-American Civil Rights Association[17] - had no problem translating the idea of 'Iron Israel' into the actual use of firearms against the enemies of the Jews. Some of his followers, members of the JDL and probably of a Chaya squad, planted a bomb in the offices of Sol Hurok, the Jewish producer who used to bring Russian artists to America. The bomb that set the place ablaze killed a young Jewish secretary who worked for Hurok.[18] It was the beginning of a series of terrorist acts which identified the behavior of the JDL and its splinter groups long after Kahane left the US. Since the mid-1970s, the American League has been consistently referred to by the FBI as a terrorist organization.

Kahane never denied his penchant for concrete violence and in his own account of the story of the Jewish Defense League, devoted a whole chapter to the justification and rationalization of JDL's violence. While making the usual argument that 'violence against *evil* is not the same as violence against *good*', and that violence for self-defense is fully legitimate, Kahane reached his famous conclusion that since Jews have been victimized for so long, 'Jewish violence in defense of Jewish interest is *never* bad'.[19] According to this theory Jewish violence is nothing but an extension of *Ahavat Isroel* (Jewish love), the natural brotherly sentiment that requires Jews to care for and help each other regardless of the conditions involved.[20]

In Israel, there was no place for further expression of 'Jewish iron', since from 1948 the country has been sovereign and Jabotinsky's notion has been realized in the Israel Defence Forces (IDF). But unlike Jabotinsky's recognized successors, Kahane apparently had not been satisfied. Though he did not establish Chaya teams in Israel, he maintained that if the state was incapable or unready to react in kind against those who spill 'so much as one drop of Jewish blood', then it was the duty of individual Israelis to do so. Slowly and without admitting that he was an ideologue of terrorism, Kahane took to legitimizing anti-Arab terror, a message fully absorbed and acted upon by his followers. One of Kahane's great historical heroes was David Raziel, the first commander of the Etzel underground in Palestine during the second half of the 1930s. It was Raziel who in 1937 introduced Jewish massive counter-terrorism against the Arabs, in opposition to the official Zionist policy of *Havlaga* (restraint). Raziel's idea, that uninvolved Arab civilians should pay for what was happening to Jewish civilians, was especially attractive to Kahane.[21] And he never cared to recognize the fact that Raziel's successors, including the admired Menachem Begin, had renounced indiscriminate terrorism already in the 1940s and became, after the establishment of the State of Israel, respectful of the law and fully confident in the Israeli Army.

In 1974 Kahane first came up with the idea of TNT (Hebrew acronym for *Terror Neged Terror* – Jewish terrorism against Arab terrorism). In

The Jewish Idea, he suggested that a 'world-wide Jewish anti-terror group' be established and that this group must be organized and aided in exactly the same way as the terrorists are aided by the Arab governments. With a totally serious face, the government of Israel must deny any connection with the group, even while allowing the same training bases on its soil as the Arab states allow the terrorists.[22] Kahane even recommended at the time the application of indiscriminate terrorism against the population of those Arab countries which provide the PLO with financial, political and military support.[23]

Kahane's idea to apply brutal Jewish counter-terrorism did not change much over the years, and in his latest book he vowed to establish, upon assuming the leadership of Israel, special Jewish anti-terror groups that would operate all over the world and help Jews wherever there is trouble, disregarding the local authorities and their laws.[24] Since the government of Israel was not receptive to his notions, Kahane's followers and other individuals inspired by his idea, soon started to act on their own. Out of fear of the Israeli police and secret services, they did not try to establish a permanent terror organization, but rather engaged in occasional anti-Arab atrocities, using the symbol of TNT.[25] Kahane's devotees were actively involved in the intensification of the conflict between Jews and Arabs in the West Bank in the 1970s. Yossi Dayan, for example, a student of Kahane and later the Secretary General of Kach, has been caught and arrested several times for provoking the Arabs in the Tomb of the Patriarchs in Hebron. In an interview he once boasted,' I had more trials than the number of stars on the American flag'.[26] Before the recent Arab uprising which has changed all the rules of public conduct in the West Bank, it was Kahane's followers who usually acted in response to Arab attacks, although by the middle of the 1980s such pretexts as acting only in reaction to Arab violence were decreasingly needed. Craig Leitner, a Kahane student, described a typical mid-1980s operation:

> One day towards the end of July 1984, I agreed with Mike Gozovsky and Yehuda Richter to operate against the Arabs. We left Kiriyat Arba in a hired car, headed towards Jerusalem . . . That night around 23.00, we went to the Neve Yaacov area. Yehuda was driving. Around midnight, we saw an Arab in his twenties walking along the road. I said 'let's stop the car'. I went out and hit the Arab with my fist on the shoulder. I also kicked him. He escaped into the night. We continued to Hebron and it was decided – I don't remember by whom – to burn Arab cars. We had in our car two plastic bottles containing four and a half litres of gasoline. In Hebron Yehuda stopped the car. Mike took the

gasoline and poured it under several cars, maybe three. Following
the burning of the cars by Yehuda, we moved, not waiting to see
what would happen. Dogs were around and I was afraid that they
would wake up the neighbors, or perhaps bite us and we would
get rabies.[27]

When asked for his reaction to the activities of Leitner and his friends,
who later fired on an Arab bus wounding several innocent passengers,
Kahane expressed total approval. He said that he was sorry that they
would have to spend years in prison and added that, in his eyes, they were
Maccabees. Later, Kahane placed Yehuda Richter, the main suspect in
the operation, as number two on his list for the Knesset. Had Kach won
two seats in 1984, Richter would have been released due to the immunity
of Israel's Knesset members. When asked once by a journalist whether
he would be willing to instruct his followers not to hit innocent Arabs
who happened to be nearby the location of a terror incident, Kahane
responded bluntly by saying, 'No, I would not. As long as they are
here we are lost. I have no way of knowing if this Arab or another
is innocent. The real danger is the demographics [the danger that the
Arabs will outnumber the Jews in Israel]'.[28]

Kach was intensely violent long before the recent Palestinian uprising.
Its entire posture, the yellow shirts with the black clenched fists, the
attacks on Arab families from within the green line (the pre-1967 Israeli
border) that move into Jewish neighborhoods, the chasing of innocent
Arab workers for the fun of it, the anti-Arab 'victory parades', the
attempts to break leftist meetings in a style reminiscent of the 1920s
Italian and German Fascists, have all spelled out hooliganism and
violence. Especially violent has been Kach's most aggressive local
stronghold, the Kiriyat Arba branch in the West Bank. Kahane's
devoted followers there have initiated since the mid-1970s countless
violent operations against the local Arabs. Unlike several Gush Emunim
activists who usually resorted to anti-Arab violence in response to
previous Arab attacks, and who said all along that they were ready to
tolerate peaceful Arab presence in the area, Kach people have never
concealed their hope for a massive emigration. The only reason for their
relative restraint has been their fear of the security forces. In 1986, and
following the intensification of Arab-Jewish violence, they established
the 'Committee for the Preservation of Security' which was to patrol the
roads in the area. But the committee that was established as a defensive
instrument against Arab rock-throwing became during the *Intifada* (the
Palestinian uprising in the West Bank and Gaza) a most aggressive
vigilante group. Its notorious commander, Shmuel Ben-Yishai, publicly

declared that any incident involving a harassment of Jewish traffic would make him shoot to kill without warning.

> I do not shoot in the air, I shoot to kill. It is stupid to fire the entire magazine in the air! Only the Jews speak about the 'purity of the arms'. Just a minute! Listen who is talking about morality: Shamir, the biggest terrorist [Itzhak Shamir, Israel's prime minister, was the commander of the Lehi terrorist underground during the 1940s]? Rabin who killed Jews on *Altalena* [a 1948 arms ship brought to Israel without official permission by the Irgun underground and destroyed by an army unit under the command of young Itzhak Rabin, Israel's 1980s minister of defence]? The Americans who murdered the Indians?[29]

In 1988 Ben-Yishai's statement was no longer an exception among the settlers of Judea and Samaria and the larger non-Kach radical right. Palestinian violence in the occupied territories has 'confirmed' what Kahane had been saying about the Arabs (and the Gentiles in general) all along. It was another attempt to 'humiliate' the Jews and to 'kill' them if possible. For most of these people it has been an indication that the decisive battle for Eretz Yisrael has already started. For a few devoted Kahane supporters it was a sign for a huge gathering storm and a possible beginning of the 'pre-redemption' catastrophe that in 1980 was predicted by Kahane to take place within about eight years.

Kahane's Sacred Violence in an Historical and Comparative Perspective

It is important to stress that Rabbi Kahane did not claim to be either a Jewish revolutionary or a religious innovator. Kahane maintained he was 'totally bound by the Halakha' and believed that in every respect, he was a genuine representative of legitimate Judaism which started with Abraham, the first Jew.[30] Whenever confronted with orthodox critics or opponents he argued that they misinterpret the authoritative texts and that he was fully ready to debate them on Halakhic grounds. But was he right? Is Kahane's revenge theology simply a reformulation of earlier Jewish theories of violence? Is it possible to explain the Kahane phenomenon by ancient or modern Jewish traditions? A careful examination of the case shows that though the leader of Kach drew upon a long line of Jewish activists, his theory of revenge is unprecedented and new. This inquiry shows further that a much stronger clue to the Kahane enigma is provided by non-Jewish expressions of his time but that even these sources do not fully explain the entire phenomenon.

The question of what should the powerless Jews do about the exile and the persecutions of the Gentiles has occasionally emerged in rabbinical deliberations since the destruction of the Second Temple (AD 70) and the Bar Kochba revolt (AD 132–135), which ended all Jewish independence in Eretz Yisrael. It was especially pressing in times of great misery when the anti-Semitic operations involved the massacre of many thousands of Jews. The major rabbinical position, which had many variations, viewed the exile as a punishment for sins committed by the nation. The creation of the Diaspora, according to these interpretations, was no chance turn of events. God's hand was directly involved in Jewish catastrophe and the Jews were expected to pay in full for their sins. The Jews were, furthermore, sworn not 'to rebel' against the Gentile nations and to wait patiently for their heavenly redemption. A prominent variation of this interpretation saw the exile as an 'ennobling punishment' and 'as proof of God's continued election of the Jews'.[31] However, there always existed a minority position which saw no holiness in passivity. While not denying God's overall responsibility for the humiliating reality of Diaspora, some medieval scholars, for example, called upon Jews to cherish historical acts of revolt and resistance such the Hasmonean rebellion, and recommended that 'When it is within our grasp, kill them'.[32]

The rise of modern Zionism involved a very dramatic challenge to the tradition of Jewish inaction, for it called upon the Jews to liberate their nation from the curse of Diaspora passivity and reassert themselves as a free people. The most radical proponent of this approach was the writer and essayist Micha Yosef Berdichevsky (1865–1921). Extremely critical of the rabbinical tradition which identified virtuous Judaism with scholarly study of the Torah and Talmudic hair splitting, Berdichevsky called for the revival of the 'Judaism of the sword'. Generations of young Zionists who were first faced with the massive anti-Jewish pogroms in eastern Europe and later with the growing violence of the Arabs in Palestine, were deeply moved by his earthly message.

> Excessive thinking drained most of our vitality, the very substance of our life. It made us too much the people of the book, too knowledgeable a nation . . . We have too much thinking, give us feeling and life, life as it really is . . .
> The best sons of the nation recognized the importance of the land for the people and fought for it gallantly. They had a living and feeling spirit . . .
> Samson who said 'let me die with the Philistines' is greater than Samson the blind, who had to escape.[33]

As early as 1907, a small Jewish organization which named itself

'Bar Giora' organized in Palestine for self defense. Originating in earlier Jewish self-defense groups which operated in Russia against the pogroms, its founders swore never to bow to Gentile aggression. In 1909 Bar Giora expanded itself into 'Hashomer' (the Watchman) which assumed the task of countering Arab violence in Palestine and securing Jewish farms and communes. This legendary organization, which remained a source of inspiration for thousands of young Zionists a long time after it was gone, adopted the motto 'Judea fell in blood and fire; in blood and fire shall Judea rise'.[34] In 1920 Hashomer transformed itself into the 'Hagana' (Defense), and became the foundation for the future Israeli Army.

While the founders of the Hagana saw their organization as the opposite quintessence of the powerless and passive ghetto Jew, their military thinking never went beyond the concept of self-defense. This was even true of Vladimir Jabotinsky, the most radical critic of the organization, who was later to become the political head of the more extreme semi-military 'Etzel' (National Military Organization in Israel). Jabotinsky, to be precise, did not like the idea of self-defense, but the reason for that had nothing to do with a theory of holy revenge. Jabotinsky was a great advocate of the legal creation of a Jewish army as a political step towards the establishment of a Jewish State in Palestine. His entire thinking about the military was legal and political.[35] Etzel's commanders in Palestine, who were not as legal and formal as their political head, were very unhappy with the concept of restrained self-defense of the Hagana, which in the second half of the 1930s provided – so they thought – an inadequate response to the growing Arab terrorism. Consequently during 1937–39 they engaged in a massive counter-terrorist campaign against the rebellious Arabs in Palestine. But in their eyes there was nothing ideological or holy about this struggle. It was a temporary, bloody, and ugly fight, the sole purpose of which was to prove that terrorism does not pay and that the Arabs were more vulnerable than the Jews.[36]

The termination of Arab terrorism in 1939 (and the beginning of the Second World War) brought an end to Etzel's terror campaign, and when the organization resumed its violent operations against the British in 1944, the logic of the fight and its practise had nothing to do with revenge or holy violence. It was perceived as a struggle for national liberation, a fight against oppression and foreign rule. Menachem Begin, the commander of Etzel and a future prime minister of Israel, explained that his decision to take up arms was not taken before all other efforts to convince the British to grant independence to the Jews failed miserably:

What use is there in writing memoranda? What value in speeches? If you are attacked by a wolf in the forest do you try to persuade him that it is not fair to tear you to pieces, or that he is not a wolf at all but an innocent lamb? Do you send him a 'memorandum'? No, there was no other way. If we did not fight we should be destroyed. To fight was the only way to salvation.

When Descartes said: 'I think, therefore I am,' he uttered a very profound thought. But there are times in the history of peoples when thought alone does not prove existence. A people may 'think' and yet its sons, with their thoughts and in spite of them, may be turned into a herd of slaves – or into soap. There are times when everything in you cries out: your very self-respect as a human being lies in your resistance to evil.

We fight, therefore we are![37]

The small 'Lehi' (Israel's Freedom Fighters), an extremist underground which in 1940 split from Etzel and immediately started to fight the British, was more radical than its parent organization. Unlike Etzel, it practised individual terrorism against the British and was determined and ruthless. It was also more traditional in its approach and on occasions referred to the Torah as its source of inspiration. But none of Lehi's ideologues had glorified revenge for the sake of revenge or saw himself as the holy avenger of Jewish blood spilled by the Gentiles for over two millenniums. Lehi's people tried, on the contrary, to ignore the existence of the Diaspora. They projected themselves as Jewish revolutionaries fighting a colonial regime in order to revive their pre-occupation commonwealth. Their concept of violence was political and was profoundly influenced by the revolutionary traditions of the Russian Narodnaya Yolia, the Italian Risorgimento, the Irish Sinn Fein, and Polish revolutionary nationalism.[38] There was certainly a revolutionary splendor in the struggle but in no way did it project a heavenly sanctified revenge. In 1943, at the height of the anti-British struggle, Itzhak Shamir, one of Lehi's head commanders and the present Israeli prime minister, explained and justified Lehi's anti-British struggle in these words:

Neither Jewish ethics nor Jewish tradition can disqualify terrorism as a means of combat. We are very far from having any moral qualms as far as our national war goes. We have before us the command of the Torah, whose morality surpasses that of any other laws in the world: Ye shall blot them out to the last man. We are particularly far from having any qualms with regard to the enemy, whose moral degradation is universally admitted here.

THE IDEOLOGIZATION OF MIMETIC DESIRE

> *But first and foremost, terrorism is for us a part of the political battle* being conducted under the present circumstances, and *it has a great part to play: speaking in a clear voice to the whole world, as well as to our wretched brethren outside this land, it proclaims our war against the occupier.*[39]

There is, thus, no question that Rabbi Kahane's expressions of violence were not isolated and that in Jewish history, especially modern, an activist strand emerged which advocated Jewish aggression and violence as part of the reassertion of the nation and its struggle for independence. But the similarity between the ideas of the major spokespersons of this school and the idiosyncratic theology of violence of the leader of Kach ends very early. While Kahane glorified in his writings the thought of Vladimir Jabotinsky, and spoke very highly of the Etzel and Lehi commanders Raziel, Stern and Begin,[40] he went far beyond their conception of legitimate violence. Not only did Kahane sanctify any anti-Gentile violence by calling it kiddush hashem, a term reserved in traditional Judaism to martyrdom, but he also made no distinction between the desired pre- and post-independence Jewish violence. Kahane intentionally ignored the fact that all his militant heroes who lived to see the establishment of the State of Israel, looked at Jewish violence as an instrument to win independence and became after 1948 non-violent Israeli citizens. And he played down the point that none of them was ever ready to disregard completely local or international law in the name of 'Jewish love'. There is clearly a cosmic element in Kahane's theology of violence, an insatiable drive for revenge which goes beyond time and space and becomes metahistorical.[41] Not a single Jew before Rabbi Meir Kahane had systematically resorted to this language and imagery.

While the review of modern Jewish activism is helpful in portraying the historical Jewish context within which the Kahane militant imagination had developed, an inquiry of the formative years of Meir Kahane in Christian America provides an additional clue to its concrete evolution. This examination shows that much of Kahane's provocative style was developed during the 1960s and was the rabbi's personal response to violent black organizations such as the SNCC (Student National Coordination Committee) and the Black Panthers. There are, in fact, many indications that as much as Kahane was outraged by the anti-Jewish and pro-Arab sentiment of the ideologues of these organizations, he was impressed by their aggressive posture and offensive language.[42] If blacks in America could challenge the white majority in the way they did, why shouldn't Jews adopt the same style towards these blacks and the

'anti-Semitic Gentiles' in general? There was a lesson to be learned from
the aggressive speeches of Stokely Carmichael and Eldridge Cleaver:

> We are talking about survival. We are talking about a people
> whose entire culture, whose entire history, whose entire way of
> life have been destroyed. We are talking about a people who have
> produced in *this* year a generation of warriors who are going to
> restore to our people the humanity and the love that we have for
> each other. That's what we are talking about *today* . . . We are
> talking about becoming the executioners of our executioners.[43]

The turbulent reality of the 1960s, in which radical students and
minority groups in America took to the streets and spoke freely about
'offing the pigs', or 'bringing down white *Amerika*', had attracted the
young rabbi and sensitized all his memories of Jewish heroism in ancient
and modern times. The ambitious young man, who had apparently been
dreaming about a great historical role in the life of his people, and
was always enchanted by aggressive behavior, had identified a golden
opportunity to make a difference.[44] Not only could he take upon the
new enemies of the Jews in a highly visible way but he could do it,
just as they did, with a large dose of aggression and violence. The
application of media-attracting violence as well as symbols like 'Jewish
Power' (vs. Black Power) which worked for the black revolutionaries
was so skillfully imitated by Kahane that he outdid in fact, all his rivals.
Between 1969 and 1971 Kahane's small JDL became one of America's
most recognized minority action groups. It was just a question of time
before its jubilant leader transformed his brand of Jewish vigilantism
into a comprehensive anti-Gentile violence and was ready to apply it
against the Russians, the Libyans, the Syrians, and potentially against
the rest of mankind.

While there is no indication that Rabbi Meir Kahane actually read the
most influential 1960s theory of violence, Franz Fanon's *The Wretched of
the Earth*, the similarity between the two ideologies is striking. The idea
that the brutal violence of the oppressed may heal their psychological
wounds, caused by years of humiliation and persecutions, was not
Kahane's. It was developed by Franz Fanon in a very elaborate way.
Although Fanon has never pronounced this violence holy, he came very
close to its glorification.

> Colonialism and imperialism have not paid their score when they
> withdraw their flags and their police forces from our territories. For
> centuries the capitalists have behaved in the underdeveloped world
> like nothing more than war criminals. Deportations, massacres,

forced labor, and slavery have been the main methods used by capitalism to increase its wealth, its gold or diamond reserves, and to establish its power.[45]

But it so happens that for the colonized people this violence, because it constitutes their only work, invests their characters with positive and creative qualities. The practice of violence binds them together as a whole, since each individual forms a violent link in the great chain, a part of the great organism of violence which has surged upward in reaction to the settler's violence in the beginning. The groups recognize each other and the future nation is already indivisible . . .

At the level of the individual violence is a cleansing force. It frees the native from his inferiority complex and from his despair and inaction; it makes him fearless and restores his self respect . . . Illuminated by violence, the consciousness of the people rebels against any pacification. From now on the demagogues, the opportunists and the magicians have a difficult task.[46]

But as appealing as a 'Fanonian' interpretation of Kahane may be, there is nevertheless a huge difference between the two, an ontological dissimilarity which far exceeds the obvious theoretical gap between the orthodox Jewish rabbi and the devoted black Marxist. Unlike Kahane's, Fanon's theory of violence is not implying cosmic struggle and does not stretch beyond time and space. It is limited to the struggle against colonialism which is expected to be over by the time all Third World nations reach independence. While Fanon's revenge sentiment is very strong, it is nevertheless political and therefore controlled. This is not the case with Rabbi Kahane. As was shown above, Kahane may have used political arguments to communicate his message, but his theology of violence was not political. Those Jews who think that the establishment of the State of Israel marks the end of holy Jewish violence, for the Israeli Army can defend the interest of the Jews routinely and legally, are wrong. It is an illusion to believe that anti-Semitism will come to an end just because the State of Israel exists. The perennial state of affairs in which the Gentiles wish to desecrate the Name of God through the humiliation and persecution of His people, is not about to change until the arrival of the Messiah and the complete redemption of the world. Consequently, Jews should constantly fight the Gentiles wherever they are. And since no Jewish violence can be wrong there is no reason to worry about legality or restraints. A Kahane-like kiddush hashem is needed now as it ever was. It is, thus, possible to conclude that neither Kahane's violent Jewish predecessors nor Franz Fanon and his followers can fully account for the Kahane phenomenon.

In Search of Meaning: The Kahane Phenomenon as the Ideologization of the Mimetic Desire

Because no Jewish or non-Jewish precedent of the past or the present seem to account for the Kahane phenomenon and since Kahane has never let anyone study his psychology or motivation from a close range, it appears that a useful way of making a general sense of the case is by applying to it some relevant psycho-literary and psycho-historical studies. René Girard's *Violence and the Sacred* provides in this respect perhaps the best intellectual tool to deal with Kahane.[47] What is useful about the Girardian methodology is not its empirical basis or wide social applicability. Girard's way of illuminating the essence of human violence does not deal with the average man or the crowd in the street. It studies instead the great mythological individuals who set in ancient times the lower and higher parameters of the human experience. The lack of direct sources drives Girard to look for them in areas social scientists rarely scan, Greek mythology and classical tragedy. Girard deals with what Max Weber would have called ideal types, pure cases and people who do not usually exist in real life but who define through their personal traits and behavior the very essence of the human condition. Many observers of Meir Kahane may not like to think of him as an historic hero and an exceptional cultural phenomenon but his personality, ideas and behavior seemed to contain the stuff of a mythological and demonic figure. His hatred of the Gentiles is greater than life and so was the intensity of his revenge theory and the extremity of his political solutions. Kahane's complete dedication to his destructive cause, despite his repeated failures and ordeals could have easily made him a literary hero of a classic Jewish tragedy were one ever written for Girard to analyze. While he would probably never had admitted that, there are many indications that the leader of Kach saw himself on occasions as the *avenging angel* of the Jewish people.

Girard's analysis of human violence, which seems particularly applicable to the Kahane case, is the theory of the mimetic desire. Violence according to Girard is a most fundamental feature of the human nature which is created and perpetuated by two basic mechanisms: *desire* and *mimesis*. Man is born with a bundle of desires, a very basic one of which is the drive to imitate the other and to obtain the same objects the other wants. Consequently, a very rudimentary conflict is created which is the root cause of all violence. The colliding desires for the same objects are bound to produce physical conflict and that violence is likely to be reproduced by the mimetic desire, the human wish to imitate the violence of the other and to destroy him by a greater dose of the same thing.

> Violent opposition, then, is the signifier of the ultimate desire, or divine self sufficiency, of that beautiful totality whose beauty depends on its being inaccessible and impenetrable. The victim of this violence both adores and detests it. He strives to master it by means of a mimetic counterviolence and measures his own stature in proportion to his failure. If by chance, however, he actually succeeds in asserting his mastery over the model, the later's prestige vanishes. He must, then, turn to an ever greater violence and seeks out an obstacle that promises to be truly insurmountable.[48]

The very origins of primitive religion are, according to Girard, the social need to reduce violence between members of the same community, who are driven by the mimetic desire to destroy each other, by providing them with surrogate victims: either sacrificial animals or humans of external societies against which their natural and reproductive violence can be directed. Only religion can control the potency of the mimetic desire, and prevent the self-destruction of the community. Religion produces myths, rituals, and taboos around the 'sacrificial crisis' that people respect and obey.

> Mimetic desire is simply a term more comprehensive than violence for religious pollution. As the catalyst for the sacrificial crisis it would eventually destroy the entire community if the surrogate victims were not at hand to halt the process and the ritualistic mimesis were not at hand to keep the conflictual mimesis from beginning afresh.[49]

An examination of Rabbi Meir Kahane in view of Girard's theory is very illuminating for it provides a conceptual context which fits both the person and the phenomenon. Kahane, the person, is the epitome of the mimetic desire. His greatest wish was to out-violate the violators of the Jews. Despite the political context of the argument there is no political thinking about this vengeance, for such thinking always implies some restraining considerations as well as some distinction between strategy and tactics. But in Kahane there is only one passion, an insatiable desire to avenge the perennial vilification of the Jews, to humiliate the Gentile, to be stronger than the other, and to demonstrate the strength by physical force. Kahane may have spoken in the name of religion but he was definitely out of its Girardian boundaries. Instead of imposing checks and controls on the violence of the community, as does Girard's primitive religion, Kahane's religion releases all safety valves. It strives to liberate the mimetic desire of the Jew, long held in judicious check by generations of Halakhic sages, and set it free. Portraying the Gentile as the epitome of anti-Jewish violence, it propagates the 'Gentilization' of the Jew so that a real revenge can take place. It calls for an eye for eye policy and preaches response in kind for thousands of years of Gentile brutality and violence.

But if Meir Kahane, the individual Jew who is determined to take revenge, fits the Girardian prototype of the mimetic desire by practising it, Rabbi Kahane, the political leader, goes beyond Girard and ideologizes the mimetic desire. Thus, what was unique about Kahane, which sets him apart from all Jewish avengers, is the elevation of the mimetic desire into a politico-religious norm. To the 'political Kahane' the 'fist in the face of the Gentile' was not simply an act of revenge, an eye for eye. It is also not a suggestion for the application of massive retaliation in kind. It is kiddush hashem, a sacred obligation all the believers, and Jews in general, are told to respect and follow. Kiddush hashem, it is important to remember, has been traditionally associated in Judaism with martyrdom, the greatest sacrifice a believer can commit, bringing about his own death in the Name of God. By ideologizing and sanctifying anti-Gentile violence, Kahane reversed Girard's primitive religion and in fact, all religion. While the function of primitive religion is to reduce tensions and to control violence, the function of Kahane's operational Judaism creates tensions and produces violence on a massive scale. The problem with this approach is that unlike all Girard's examples which are either taken from Greek tragedy or tribal anthropology, Kahane's theology is real and is practised in Israel in the last years of the twentieth century.

NOTES

1. Rabbi Meir Kahane, 'hillul hashem', (A Kach mimeographed article, n.d.-Hebrew). Kahane was assassinated in New York City on 5 Nov. 1990.
2. On Gush Emunim, see Gideon Aran, 'From Religious Zionism to Zionist Religion: The Roots of Gush Emunim and Its Culture' (Unpublished Doctoral Dissertation, Hebrew University of Jerusalem, 1987-Hebrew); David Newman, ed., *The Impact of Gush Emunim* (London: Croom Helm, 1985); Zvi Raanan, *Gush Emunim* (Tel Aviv: Sifriyat Poalim, 1980-Hebrew); Danny Rubinstein, *On the Lord's Side: Gush Emunim* (Tel Aviv: Hakibbutz Hameuchad, 1982-Hebrew); Ehud Sprinzak, 'Gush Emunim: The Iceberg Model of Political Extremism', *Medina Mimshal Yeyehasim Beinleumiim*, No. 17, (Fall 1981-Hebrew); 'Gush Emunim: The Politics of Zionist fundamentalism in Israel', (New York, NY: The American Jewish Committee, 1986); for a recent review of the Gush Emunim literature, see Eliezer Don-Yehiya, 'Jewish

Messianism, Religious Zionism and Israeli Politics: The Impact and Origins of Gush Emunim', *Middle Eastern Studies*, Vol. 23, No. 2, (April 1987), pp.215–34.
3. On the strong anti-Gentile motive in Kahane's thinking, see Aviezer Ravitzky, 'The Roots of Kahanism: Consciousness and Political Reality', *The Jerusalem Quarterly* No. 39, 1986.
4. Kahane, *Listen World, Listen Jew* (Tucson, AZ: The Institute of Jewish Idea, 1975), pp.121–22.
5. Cf. George Sorel, *Reflections on Violence* (New York, NY: Collier, 1961); Franz Fanon, *The Wretched of the Earth* (New York, NY: Grove Press, 1968).
6. Cf. Gerald Cromer, 'The Debate About Kahanism In Israeli Society 1984–1988', *Occasional Papers* (New York, NY: The Harry Frank Guggenheim Foundation, 1988), p.35.
7. In his *The Story of the Jewish Defense League* (Radnor, PA: Chilton Book Company, 1975), Kahane has a special chapter titled: 'Violence: Is This Any Way For a Nice Jewish Boy To Behave?', in which he provides the rationale for the violence of the American Jewish Defense League. The reader is told that among its other purposes, 'Jewish violence is meant to . . . Destroy the Jewish neuroses and fears that contribute so much encouragement to the anti-Semite as well as Jewish belief in his own worthlessness. We want to instill self-respect and self-pride in a Jew who is ashamed of himself for running away', p.142.
8. Cf. Howard M. Sachar, *A History of Israel* (Jerusalem: Steimatzky, 1976), pp.14–15, 38–41.
9. Kahane, *Never Again: A Program for Jewish Survival* (New York, NY: Pyramid Books, 1972), pp.74–101.
10. Ibid., 'The Anti-Semites', pp.72–104.
11. Ibid., 'Zionism', pp.151–74.
12. Cf. Kahane, *Israel's Eternity and Victory* (Jerusalem: The Institute of Jewish Idea, 1973-Hebrew); *Numbers 23:9* (Jerusalem: The Institute of Jewish Idea, 1984-Hebrew).
13. Kahane, *Forty Years* (Miami, FL: Institute of the Jewish Idea, 1983), pp.6–7.
14. According to Kahane's deterministic logic, the only condition for complete salvation is a full repentance of the entire nation. His expected takeover of political power may have been a big step in the right direction, but since he did not plan to impose a forced repentance on the entire people, it would 'probably not satisfy God'. He would have tried to tell the people about the disaster that awaited them but if they chose not to listen then even he would be unable to save them. Author's interview with Kahane, 12 June 1988.
15. Kahane, *The Story of the Jewish Defense League*, pp.278–79. Janet L. Dolgin, *Jewish Identity and the JDL*, (Princeton, NJ: Princeton University Press, 1977), Ch.3.
16. Kahane, *The Story of the Jewish Defense League*, pp.99–100.
17. For Kahane's own account of this strange association see, Rabbi Meir Kahane, ibid. pp.185–91.
18. Cf. Yair Kotler, *Heil Kahane* (Tel Aviv: Modan, 1985-Hebrew), pp.103–8. Kahane never bothered to apologize for the killing of the innocent secretary. Instead he complains in his book on the JDL about the refusal of the Jewish establishment to bail out the three JDL youngsters accused of 'Jewish political crime'. Kahane, *The Story of the Jewish Defense League*, p.191.
19. Ibid., pp.141–42.
20. Ibid., pp.75–80.
21. Cf. Kahane, 'hillul hashem', p.3; *Listen World, Listen Jew*, pp.88–89; *From the Knesset Stand: The Speeches of Rabbi Kahane in the Knesset* (Jerusalem: Kach Movement, n.d.-Hebrew), p.11.
22. Kahane, *The Jewish Idea*, p.14.
23. Kahane, 'hillul hashem', p.3.
24. Cf. Kahane, *Uncomfortable Questions For Comfortable Jews*, (Secaucus, NJ: Lyle Stuart, 1987), p.269.

25. Since May 1975 the initials TNT have occasionally surfaced following mysterious attacks on Arab institutions in Jerusalem. A small group that called itself TNT was arrested in 1975 after setting two Arab buses on fire. Cf. *Yediot Achronot* 18 June 1975. Threat letters sent to Arab leaders were also signed by TNT. In Dec. 1983 there was another series of sabotage acts in Jerusalem associated with TNT. Cf. Yakir Tzur, 'Military Background, Expertise in Sabotage and Extremist Ideology', *Kol Hair*, 16 Dec. 1983.
26. Quoted in Kotler, *Heil Kahane*, p.257.
27. Quoted in Nadav Shragai, 'Going for the Action', *Ha'aretz*, 27 Nov. 1984.
28. Quoted in Haim Shibi, 'Wherever There is Blood Spilled You Find Kahane', *Yediot Achronot*, 2 Aug. 1985.
29. Yair Avituv, 'All is Well in the Kasba', *Kol Hair*, 12 Aug. 1988.
30. This is based on numerous talks and interviews I have personally conducted with Kahane.
31. David Biale, *Power and Powerlessness in Jewish History* (New York, NY: Schocken Books, 1987), pp.37–38.
32. Quoted by Biale, ibid, p.38.
33. Cf. Micha Yosef Ben-Gurion (Berdichevsky), *Collected Essays* (Tel Aviv: Dvir, 1951), p.47.
34. Quoted in Ian Lustick, 'Solipsistic Terrorism in the Arab-Israeli Conflict' (Draft paper presented at the Ford Foundation Conference on Terrorism, Wesleyan University, May 1989), p.5.
35. On Jabotinsky's ideas about the need for a Jewish army as well as about revolt and violence, see Yaacov Shavit, *The Mythologies of the Right* (Beit Berl: the Sharett Institute, 1985-Hebrew), Ch.3.
36. Cf. David Niv, *The Battle for Freedom; The Etzel* (Tel Aviv: The Klausner Institute, 1975-Hebrew), Part II, pp.40–42.
37. Menachem Begin, *The Revolt* (Tel Aviv: Steimatzky, 1951), p.46.
38. Cf. Joseph Heller, *Lehi: Ideology and Politics, 1940–1949* (Jerusalem: Keter, 1989-Hebrew), pp.151–57.
39. Itzhak Shamir quoted in Ian Lustick, 'Solipsistic Terrorism in the Arab-Israeli Conflict', pp.10–11.
40. Kahane's admiration for the commanders of Etzel and Lehi has been expressed in many books of his, see, for example, Kahane, *Never Again*, pp. 163–74.
41. On the element of cosmic struggle in religious violence, see Mark Juergensmeyer, 'The Logic of Religious Violence' in David Rapoport (ed.), *Inside Terrorist Organizations* (London: Frank Cass, 1988), pp.185–90, and his essay in this volume.
42. Cf. Kahane's obsession with the Black extremists of the 1960s has been expressed in many of his articles and books. See, for example, references to Stokely Carmichael and Eldridge Clever in Kahane, *The Story of the Jewish Defense League*, pp.64–69; 199–203; and also Ch.6 (Jewish Power).
43. Stokely Carmichael, 'A Declaration of War', in Massimo Teodori (ed.), *The New Left: A Documentary History*, (Indianapolis, Bobbs Merill, 1969), pp. 281–82.
44. Cf. Michael T. Kaufman, 'The Complex Past of Meir Kahane', *The New York Times*, 24 Jan. 1971, pp.1, 51.
45. Franz Fanon, *The Wretched of the Earth*, p.101.
46. Ibid, pp.93–95.
47. René Girard, *Violence and the Sacred*, (Baltimore, MD: The Johns Hopkins University Press, 1977).
48. Ibid, p.148.
49. Ibid.

The Mythologies of Religious Radicalism: Judaism and Islam

EMMANUEL SIVAN

At the height of the Salman Rushdie affair (February–March 1989) my favorite Haredi (Jewish ultra-conservative) weekly, *Bamahane Hararedi*, consecrated to it at least one page per issue with sensational headlines to boot. Coverage was overtly empathetic – even sympathetic with Khomeini's stand. Analogies were drawn between Rushdie and Jewish blasphemers (including a recent Israeli play entitled *Comrades Talking about Jesus*). The fight against blasphemy of things religious is one and the same, declared a leading Haredi rabi; a like-minded member of Knesset added that Khomeini had set an example which the faithful of Judaism had better follow if they want to cleanse Israel from the dross of the 'new idolatry', that is, Jewish adepts of Western materialism, profanation, and hedonism.

This was a rare, but quite illuminating manifestation of mimetic desire[1] in operation between radical movements of two, often adversarial religions. All the more illuminating as the matter did not stop there. Inspired (or emboldened) by the Rushdie affair, the Haredi disciples of 92-year-old Rabbi A. M. Schach launched in the following summer a virulent campaign against Rabbi Adin Steinsaltz. The latter, a conservative fundamentalist, made his reputation as past master of upmarket popularizing of Jewish traditional lore destined to win hearts and minds among secular Israelis. He has become a media celebrity, consulted as guru by intellectuals, politicians and generals attracted to his (externally modernized) version of the fundamentalist gospels. The ultra-conservatives suspected (or is it that they envied?) him for years, whereas he straddled the religious and secular segments of society. But only in July–August 1989 did they find the nerve to brand him in public as a Rushdie-style apostate (*meshumad*, in Hebrew; the Islamic term is *murtadd*). The evidence cited came from books written a decade ago where he ventured, lo and behold, some mild criticism of a few biblical figures. These books were banned by the rabbis and ultimately buried in public in ditches dug specially for that purpose (one does not burn books, in Judaism, if God's name appears therein). Whereas the ultra-conservatives occupy the moral high ground among religious Jews, poor Rabbi Steinsaltz had to go to Canossa. He made a public *mea culpa*, took all extant copies of these books out of circulation, vowed to reissue an expurgated edition, and solemnly undertook never to perpetrate again this 'terrible oversight' as he chose to call it.

Conservative Jews are indeed so harried by ultra-conservative vituperations on their laxity that they endeavor to prove their own zeal by chasing other deviations from the traditional version of Sacred History. Their representative in the Higher Broadcasting Authority demanded, for instance, in late September 1990, to revamp (or if not, to ban) a teleplay commissioned by the state-run television, where King David is said to be depicted as 'an adulterer, a fickle minded adventurer; solely involved in satisfying his personal desires and ambitions'. At the time of writing, the Steinsaltz and King David affairs – both holding the Rushdie example as role model – have not yet been laid to rest.

For an analogous case of such mimetic desire in Islam, one should go back to Sunni students' publications in the 1970s, where the establishment of the state of Israel was cited as telling proof that a 'religious renaissance' can have an impact in the modern world, albeit in a national guise, win wars, employ modern technology, and maintain a viable state permeated by a reinvogorated religious tradition.[2] Other radical varieties in these two religions are totally oblivious to the temptations of the mimetic desire. Gush Emunim says nothing in like vein of the Hamas movement, the major opponent of its settlers. And as for Shiite Iran, it never breathed a word as to its possible intrinsic affinity with the Haredis who so admire it.

The reason for the rarity of such expressions of similiarity due to conflict, or of 'two desires converging on the same object [that] are bound to clash', in Girard's famous formula, is quite evident. Jewish and Islamic radicalism is interested, above all, in saving its own respective culture from the insidious danger of apostates from within, rather than from attacks by infidels from without. The Arab-Israeli, or Muslim-Jewish, political conflict, is secondary. The external enemy is to be tackled only after internal enemies, false ('hypocritical') Muslims or Jews, are subjugated. Remarkably, though, whenever Muslim and Jewish fundamentalists find themselves, by dint of circumstances, locked in a direct clash, the dynamics charted by Girard, surface unmistakably. Thus a kabbalistic guru, Rabbi Isaac Kedourie, reacted to the *Intifada*, by suggesting that in order to achieve peace with the Arabs, 'one should sacrifice a scapegoat – the Gaza Strip – which is barely part and parcel of Eretz Yisrael, and thus avoid further bloodshed'. A Palestinian state in Gaza, an idea broached even by some Gush Emunim rabbis, is presented as the sort of sacrifice which may put an end to the Girardian chain reaction of vengeance; for what is vengeance if not violence born out of similarity (desire for the same object, *p. ex.*, Eretz Yisrael/Palestine) which, once breaking out of control, spawns an even greater similarity, each murderous act performed in the same way for the same reasons in vengeful imitation of the preceding murder.

In like manner the leaflets of the Hamas insurgency in Gaza speak for *internal* consumption of Palestine as the 'Promised Land' *al-watan al-maw'ud* of Islam, a term which has no basis in Muslim tradition and is evidently copied from the Zionist religio-political vocabulary. Zealot preachers of Hizbollah in southern Lebanon depict the sacrifice enjoined by God upon Abraham as one referring to Ishmael, not to Isaac. They may be trying here not only to present a sort of Muslim counter-version to the biblical story (a counter-version outlined by medieval commentators such as al-Tabari, al-Kisa'i, and al-Tha'alibi, writing on *Qur'an* Ch.37: 97–113); they may also be concocting a counter-myth, one which tries to subvert and expropriate the Zionist religio-political one (born in 1930 and sacralized by the 1948 war) regarding the 'new sacrifice of Abraham': the generation of Zionist parents sacrificing their (willing – even enthusiastic) sons in order to regain Eretz Yisrael. Not so, intimate the Hizbollah preachers, the original (intended) sacrifice was that of Ishmael, the forefather of the Arabs; the present (real) sacrifice is that of his descendants, the Lebanese Arab suicide-bombers of Hizbollah.[3]

It should be emphasized that these cases are few and far between. The two radical movements are essentially inner-oriented, even if their actions, as in the case of Gush Emunim, spawn violence against unbelievers.

And yet, probing affinities between varieties of religious radicalism is not a futile exercise. For what is religious radicalism? One can define it as a mode of thought and action which consists, first of all, of the rejection of surrounding cultural forms and values that are not perceived as endogenous (or authentic) to the religious tradition; and, second, in order to bolster this rejection, certain key components of this tradition have to be reinvigorated and intensified.[4] For this excess, the notion that 'the more is the better', is the essence of radicalism or extremism, it is never excess for its own sake. The violence to which they have recourse – be it verbal or physical – is never violence for its own sake. Excess and violence serve a higher goal – the defense of a tradition deemed to be under siege. Radicalism is, for that reason, inextricably linked to the nature of the specific religious tradition as well as to the character of the challenge. The radical may very well differ from the rest of the believers of that religion just by the emphasis he puts on a certain aspect of that tradition, even as he continues to share with them a worldview or a meaning system. He also differs from them, of course, by an acute perception of the danger(s) lurking either from within or from without.

The study of radicalism is, therefore, part and parcel of the comparative study of religion. To study the extremist forms of one religion alongside (or, if possible, in comparison with) those of another religion may enable us to highlight not only similarities but also differences between the two.

The essential impulse shared by all Jewish and Islamic radicals is what one may dub, 'innovative traditionalism', i.e., a political radicalism born out of a religious tradition, which transcends that tradition in an attempt to preserve its authenticity in the face of contemporary challenges. The tradition defended thereby is not a matter of desiccated bookish lore, nor is it a marginal component (or a set of long forgotten precedent) in the history of that religion. In all the movements we deal with it as a living tradition, transmitted from one generation to another by scholars, mystics or other religious activists, and one which is part and parcel of the mainstream of that religion.

Sunni and Shiite radicalism was born out of an anti-accommodative attitude towards political power which had always existed within these two strands of Islam. This attitude was much more important in Shiite Islam, given its persecuted stance throughout history. But even among the Sunni, who are, on the whole, more accommodative, there has always been a legitimate, vigilante-type alternative which was definitely anti-accommodative and was perceived as being within the pale, an integral part of Sunni political lore. Some of this vigilante lore has been covered by historical dust (for example, the writings of the school of Ibn Hazm in Muslim Spain), but other variants continued to exist to this day (namely, the neo-Hanbalite school founded by Ibn Taymiyya in the fourteenth century). When modern Sunni radicals looked in the 1960s for a tradition to build upon, they naturally turned to Ibn Taymiyya. Neither here, nor in Shiite Islam does the phenomenon in any way represent a case of heresies raising their heads, outside the pale of the legitimate religious discourse. All attempts made by the Egyptian regime, to brand radicals as heretics (*p. ex.*, as Kharijites or Qaramats) inevitably failed.

Heresy is likewise definitely not what Jewish radicalism consists of. The ultra-orthodoxy of the Haredim and the *Neturei Karta* is a successor to a long tradition of Jewish exclusionary life in the Diaspora; a tradition which until the Age of Enlightenment and secular nationalism (even up to the Holocaust) was *the* major living tradition of Judaism, resigned to life outside of history (and outside of politics) as long as God has not performed the miracle of Messianic redemption. As for Gush Emunim, they build upon the minor, but legitimate tradition of Jewish activist Messianism – exerting oneself to hasten the arrival of the Messiah and not just passively waiting for him – a tradition that has played a key role in certain historical moments as late as the seventeenth century (such as the mass movement of Shabtai Zvi with its deep roots in the Kabbalah). These medieval cabbalistic concepts were revamped by Rabbi Zvi Yehuda Kook, Jr. in the 1950s in order to answer questions raised by the establishment of the state of Israel, in a manner no different in essence than the one used by Sunni thinker Sayyid Qutb to reinterpret the Ibn Taymiyya political theory for the needs of the twentieth century. In a slightly different fashion, this is also what Khomeini did to *usuli* notion of ulama hierarcy and social responsibility.

It should be stressed that the different traditions they build upon explain the divergent paths of Sunni and Shiite religio-political movements today. Despite all the 'ecumenic' attempts at *rapprochement*, their paths are likely to remain as divergent as ever.

The divergence of opinion between Gush Emunim and the Haredim is not so much a matter of basic concepts as both accept the distinction between 'normal', Diasporic time perspective and miraculous, Messianic time perspective – as much as a matter of diagnosis. The Gush considers that the Messianic Age of Redemption actually dawned in 1948, the Haredim still consider that they live in a Diasporic age, the establishment of the 'apostate' state of Israel having changed nothing.

It is their strong base in the religious tradition that goes far to explain the initial appeal that all these movements have for 'true believers'. This base is also what makes the believers' task of transcending the living tradition, while remaining true to it, so complex and daunting. For, despite their deep roots in tradition, these cannot be called conservative movements, as they spring from a radical political mythology designed to galvanize people into political action aimed at delegitimizing and eventually scuttling the political and/or social order.[5] In the case of 'innovative traditionalism', the intellectual and affective justification for the myth – a dramatic story based on past or future events, either true or fictional – is found not in a long-extinguished or brand-new set of values, but in values still cherished by some parts of society.

These values provide the radicals with a set of criteria for judging the present state of affairs as nefarious, whereas the primordial impulse of all these radical movements is one of religiosity in a state of siege, i.e., a defensive initiative designed to thwart the demise of either Judaism or Islam, undermined from within by 'nominal (hypocritical) believers', who are in fact Hellenized (*mityavnim*, in Hebrew), Westoxicated (*gharbzadaga*, in Persian, *mustashriqun*, in Arabic). All these terms, and their plethora of synonyms, refer in Sunni, Shiite, and Jewish ultra-orthodox militancy to one and the same phenomenon – people captivated by the ideas of the Age of Enlightenment in the broadest sense of the term (man-centered, progress-minded, scientific, rationalist, etc). In the case of Gush Emunim the modernity which is rejected is of a more constricted type – secular Zionism with its 'defeatist propensity' for compromise over immutable values such as the sanctity of the Land of Israel; a propensity 'laid bare' after the 1973 war. In all four movements, however, the tools of modernity are accepted (be they media, technology, military hardware, and so forth); rejection refers to goals and values – not to means.

As befits religions predicated upon Divine Law, the Jewish and Islamic extremist militants deduce these goals and values from the *Halakha* and the *Shari'a*. And the Law also provides guidelines for the construction of the future order – 'a Halakh state' or 'a Shari'a" state'; these slogans heralded by Haredis as well as by Sunnis and Shiites, refer to an ideal polity in which the religious code covers the public as much as the private place, and usually according to the most rigorous exegesis, the obverse of the lenient one resorted to by the modernist reformers. Here again, Gush Emunim differs from all the rest: it concentrates the application of Halakha on one major issue: the annexation of the 'still unredeemed' parts of the Land of Israel – the territories governed *de facto* by the Jewish State.

This characteristic is closely associated with the unique diagnosis in which the *Gush* believes, i.e., the establishment of Israel as heralding the advent of Redemption. The interplay between the legal and the Messianic is here quite evident. For Jews, the Jewish State can be achieved only outside the historical time-perspective. This is the reason why the ultra-orthodox who do not see the End of Days on the horizon, deny the legitimacy of the State of Israel (established in 1948) and aspire to re-establish the Diasporic type of closely-knit, Halakha-governed, autonomous community that had existed in the eastern European *Shtetl*. The past they are fixated on – that is, their 'myth of foundation' (in anthropological parlance) – is the seventeenth and eighteenth centuries when the Shtetl flourished. (This is why they are clad in the black garb so common in eighteenth century Poland.) The only exception to this anti-Messiamic rule is the *Habad* (Lubavitcher) Hassidic sect which believes that the process of redemption may begin any moment and look for annotiatory signs ('the pangs of Messiah'). Many of them even speculate, with evident inner tension, that the current holder of the mantle of the Lubavitcher Rebbe may be the Messiah.

The Gush Emunim ultra-nationalists legitimize and sacralize the State of Israel precisely because they believe that its very existence is proof that the process of Redemption has begun and that we are therefore already operating outside history. But, for the ultra-nationalists, Israel can only fulfil its destiny if certain conditions related to Messianic requirements – e.g., the settlement of the Land of Israel which is the theater of Redemption – are met. Thus the activity of these Jewish radicals is mainly geared towards furthering the process of Redemption by settling the entire land. Their 'founding myth' is, accordingly, fixated on a completely different past – the first and the second Jewish Commonwealths (thirteenth to sixth centuries BC; second century BC to second century AD), which prefigure the third Commonwealth which is now being created through the 'pangs of the Messianic Redemption'. It is no coincidence that the Gush activists are dressed in unabashedly contemporary Israeli grab, with a dash of pioneering, military accoutrement. The skullcap and ostentatiously-worn prayer shawl are the sole vestimentary signs of their Messianic obsessions. They speak modern Hebrew while the Haredis prefer Yiddish, the day to day language of the Shtetl (Hebrew being the sacred language of Ritual and Law). The Gush pick fancy Biblical names for their offspring and settlements, the Haredis opt for common 'Diasporic' ones.

The interplay between Messianism, legal ideals, and myths of the past is operating along different lines in radical Islam. The Messianic element is tightly held in abeyance in almost all Sunni groups, the only exception being the Sunni sect Takfir wa-Hijra in 1977 Egypt, which declared its leader (who was later executed) as the Mahdi (Messiah) and caliph. But, unlike the ultra-nationalist Gush Emunim, this sect was antinomian (not unlike the medieval Qarmats) in that it also rejected most of the Shari'a as evil because its evolution throughout Islamic history had always been contaminated by collusion with the powers-that-be. The exception just proves the rule. The Messianic element is on the whole quite irrelevant to the Sunni discourse on delegitimation. Sunni radicals hold that the present order must be toppled in 'normal' (non-Messianic) historical time and a new legitimate order established without awaiting the new Messiah or Mahdi.

In this stance Sunni radicals are true heirs to the Sunni tradition where there is indeed a belief in a Messiah who would come, at the End of Time, and after a struggle with the Antichrist will establish the realm of justice upon earth. But not only was this belief quite secondary, it has become in the course of the centuries even marginal. The

great eleventh-century theologian al-Ghazali passes it in silence, while
the famous philosopher of history Ibn Khaldun (fourteenth century)
subjected it to a scathing critique.

Belief in the apocalypse was typical, though by no means prominent,
among Sufis (mystics) and even there the context was in general quietistic
– knowing that the Messiah was due to come enabled one to forbear
suffering and injustice, sit tight and do nothing but pray. While in the
first two centuries of Islam there were Sunni apocalyptic revolts, this
tradition was soon taken over and almost completely monopolized by
the Shiah (or to be more precise: by its Ismaili and Imamite branches).
The few such Sunni revolts in later times – the most famous among
which is that of the 'Mahdi' in Sudan (1880–81) – erupted in peripheral
Islamic countries, in an anti-colonial context, and were the product of
a sub-culture of marginal mystics and preachers. Such a sub-culture
was soon to be completly erased by modernization and with it died
out much of the spirit of apocalyptic activism.[6] Contrary to what the
Arab Left expected, then, Messianism did not become the mainstay of
a revolutionary tradition in the lands of Islam.[7]

It goes differently for the Shiite, especially the majority Imamite sect
with its belief in a Hidden (twelfth) Imam, 'in occultation' since 941 and
due to come back upon Earth on Judgement Day and re-establish the
rule of the House of Ali as well as the perfect application of Islamic
law, and, hence, the rule of justice – as a vindication of Shiite suffering
throughout history.

This is a major Shiite myth whereas the precept of *Raja* (return
to Earth) of the Hidden Imam is accepted by most Shiites – with the
exception of a few ecumenic thinkers[8] who wish not to hurt Sunni
sensibilities – as a fundamental tenet. Yet the notion of a Hidden Imam
operated from the early tenth century above all in a quietistic context.
After all, the very use of this idea among Twelver (Imamite) Shiites was
associated with the time of the worst Abbasid persecutions and tended
to thwart Shiites from virtually suicidal insurrections, recommending to
suffer in silence and bide their time. This was its major function through
most Imamite history. Indeed most of the important Shiite revolutionary
movements came from the Ismaili branch (*p.ex.*, the Qarmats where the
Mahdi was always steeped in an activistic lore with anti-proclivities).

Khomeini did not try his hand in infusing activism into Iranian beliefs
in the Mahdi, judging, quite sensibly, that there was no great apocalyptic
tension to be energized among the masses. In his major work, *Islamic
Government* (1971) he criticizes the many Shiites who collaborate with
the authorities based upon the premise that man must strive to achieve
justice in the here and now, in this world from which the Imam is

absent, and not wait 'hundreds and perhaps even thousands of years' for the establishment of absolute justice by the Imam upon his return to Earth. However, even if Khomeini did not stress the concept of Imam (or the Mahdi), his teaching repeatedly implied the principle that forms the boundary of the time-frame in which he worked (the fifth article of the Iranian constitution states that it will be valid 'as long as the Twelfth Imam is absent'). Furthermore, Khomeini served as a *marja* (highest religious authority) since the early 1960s, and his authority as such was defined as stemming from a delegation of authority for the sake of guardianship (*wilaya amma*) on behalf of the Hidden Imam. Only in this way could Khomeini transform the institution of *marja* from a strictly religious function into one that is political as well. Some of his adepts who were inclined to literal interpretations would even claim that Khomeini was actually a mystical emanation issuing directly from the Mahdi and serving as vanguard for the Mahdi's return.

It is from this concept that the title applied to Khomeini – but not yet to his successor Ali Khamenei – *naib al-Imam* (vicar of the Hidden Imam) – is derived. Khomeini did try to emphasize that he was not imbued with the Hidden Imam's spiritual powers (especially not with *isma*, infallibility), and that since in essence he was not different from other mortals, his rule was strictly functional (*wilaya i'tibariyy*). Nonetheless, the frame of reference and the basis for comparison is the Mahdi: the regime is measured against him, and the time allotted for it to rule is delimited by his eventual return. This is an important pillar of Khomeini's worldview, though not as crucial as *wilyat al-faqih*. It should therefore come as no surprise that the Hidden Imam's birthday (which falls on the 15th of Shaban) has always been one of the four major religious holidays in Iran (along with the Ashura and the birthdays of Ali and Husain, all relate to the 'foundation myth'). During this holiday, Khomeini extolled the 'return of the Imam-Mahdi in the End of the Days' in fervid speeches that received wide media coverage.

Eschatology is thus present in Shiite mythology but in a different fashion then in Gush Emunim: no fervent expectation of an imminent End of Days, no computations of the expected date based on signs and miracles, no reading of any crisis (such as the *Intifada*) as part and parcel of the 'pangs of redemption', no temptation 'to force God's hand' and hasten the Redemption (as in the case of the Jewish underground). It is true that at the affective level the Shiites do retain an eschatological undercurrent, nevertheless it is the Sharia myth, with its clear cut orientation towards the past, which definitely reigns supreme even among the Shiites, especially as the interpreters of the law, the ulama, lead the Shiite radicals and, in fact, constitute the revolutionary cadre.

It follows, then, that the Sunni, Shiite, and Jewish ultra-orthodox myths are essentially past-orientated in that they focus upon eras in which the Divine Law was effectively applied in 'normal' historical time – the seventh century for the Muslims and the seventeenth and eighteenth centuries for the Shtetl time for the Jews (the Lubavitcher sect is the Haredi exception, being past- and future-orientated). The ultra-nationalist Jewish myth is orientated towards both the past (the two Jewish Commonwealths) and the future of the Jewish state, insofar as it will apply the law (Halakha) in accordance with tradition.

The functions of political myths are not merely cognitive and hermeneutic – interpreting past, present, and future and therby defining group identity – but also behavioral. In other words, myths are supposed to lead to action. But whether action will be directed towards drawing away from the corrupt present order into a state of internal or physical exile, or toward taking the initiative to change the present state of affairs by whatever means are at hand – including violence – depends on the circumstances. Still, there is here again a broad common denominator between Jewish ultra-nationalists, most Sunni and all Shiite radicals: all three rely on deliberate intervention in the socio-political arena to bring about change in the 'apostate' rulers and civil society of their own camp and, if necessary, in foreign powers as well. Ultra-orthodox Jews, on the other hand, defer all structural change to Messianic times, and the few Sunni sects (such as the Samawiyya in Egypt) that despair of ever being able to defy the all-powerful modern nation-state, retire into a self-imposed seclusion designed to save their own soul even if they cannot save the 'apostate', hostile, and alien environment in which they are fated to live.

But, whether they choose withdrawal or activism, both Jewish and Islamic radicals endeavor to preserve their own versions of the tradition they cherish by constructing 'counter-societies'[10] predicated upon values and patterns of behavior alien and inimical to their civil societies. These 'counter-societies' serve two purposes. They are designed to serve as models for a future society based upon the rigorous application of either Sharia or Halakha and in the case of the more 'interventionist' minded radicals, they also view themselves as potential tools for subverting and toppling the present order.

This accounts for the Haredi sustained effort to maintain their distance from the 'Zionist apostate state', by relying on the funding from sympathizers in the Diaspora in order to maintain their own network of services (particularly in education, health, and welfare but also in internal policing work; while having recourse for the services of the accursed state only *in extremis* (for example, for external security). In like fashion, the Sunni radicals in Egypt, Tunisia and Sudan – chastened by the recent failure of their revolutionary attempts – rely today more and more on developing near their mosques out-patient clinics and educational establishments (including pre-school, a novelty in Arab lands). Through these institutions – as well as through Islamic Banks where usury is prohibited – they hope to minimize their followers' contact with the state and prove that Islamic ideals of social justice and moral probity can be implemented in a modern setting.

The toppling of the present order remains the goal – however remote and elusive – of all radicals surveyed in this essay. For the 'interventionalist'-minded this involves the possibility of active martyrdom, while passive martyrdom is all that can be envisaged for those who practice withdrawal, be they Sunnis or ultra-orthodox Jews. The underlying motivation for both modes of behavior is an alienation which, while it is to some extent intellectual, is mainly emotional. It is to this alienation that the radicals not only aspire, but have generally succeeded in, disseminating among both their own hardcore and in their ever-expanding periphery. That is how they come to exercise effective cultural hegemony in their respective societies.

NOTES

1. R. Girard, *Violence and the Sacred* (Baltimore, MD and London: The Johns Hopkins University Press, 1977), Ch.5. The formula which we quote *infra*, p.3 is taken from the same book, p.146, and cf. ibid., pp.147–51. The notion of sacrificial scapegoat discussed below (p.3) is indebted to Girard's *Things Hidden Since the Foundation of the World* (1987).
2. *Nazarat Muasira fi Tarikhina* (Muslim Students' Association, University of Cairo, 1975). This concept was first spelt out in the early 1950s by thinkers associated with the Muslim Brothers such as Muhammad al-Ghazali.
3. *Yom Ha-Shishi* (Jerusalem), 13 Oct. 1989; *Nekuda* (Gush Emunim), 30 June 1989, pp.50–1; Sheikh Raghib Harb, *al-Minbar al-Muqawim* (Beirut: 1988), pp.92, 159.
4. C.S. Liebman, 'Extremism as a Religious Norm', *Journal for the Scientific Study of Religion*, Vol.22, No.7 (1983).
5. See H. Tudor, *Political Myth* (London, 1972); L.P. Thompson, *The Political Mythology of Apartheid* (New Haven, CT: 1985); D. Kertzer, *Ritual, Politics and Power*.
6. P. Von Sivers, 'The Realm of Justice', *Humaniora Islamica* 1 (1973).
7. M.A. al-Alim, *Dirasat fi-l-Islam* (Beirut: 1981).
8. M. Kashif al-Ghita', *Asl al-Shia wa-Usuliha*, 10th ed. (Beirut: 1958), p.128.
9. E. Kohlberg, 'From Imamiyya to Ithna-Ashariyya' *BSOAS* (1975) pp.521–34; A.A. Sachedina, *Islamic Messianism* (Albany, NY: 1981).
10. Cf. A. Kriegel, *The French Communists* (Chicago, IL: 1972), introduction.

The Islamic Idiom of Violence:
A View from Indonesia

BRUCE B. LAWRENCE

Violence has often been discussed as the motive or consequence of a religiously-coded repertoire of words and deeds, rhetoric and ritual merging, then unfolding in myriad ways into the lived experience of religious actors. René Girard has moved the discussion to a new level of insight through his examination of textual narratives common to what George Steiner once called the Judaic-Hellenistic canon. Yet Islam remains extraneous to that canon; the scriptures, judicial conventions, and historical experience of Muslims come into consideration only as the second order reading of categories shaped by others' data.

In trying to link Girardian hypotheses with Islamic evidence, one may consider a spectrum of possible interpretive moves: (1) to locate Islamic rhetoric within phenomenological discourse about religion, stressing pre-modern features of tribal or segmentary societies as definitive of Islamic norms that encode honor yet also promote violence; (2) to demonstrate the overlap between religious and political affinities to violence in nearly all judicial systems, Islamic and non-Islamic, but also in revivalist movements masking, as they often do, political objectives in religious rhetoric; or (3) to trace themes of sacrifice and martyrdom as inscribed, memorialized, and now ritualized by some present-day Muslim groups, especially those who have been socially displaced and economically marginalized by the late capitalist world system. Each of these interpretive moves has been developed, and ably advanced, by other contributors to this volume. Mark Anspach develops the first, David Rapoport and Emmanuel Sivan the second, while Martin Kramer dramatizes the third.

Rather than embrace any one or a combination of these three moves, I choose to locate my own investigation in a fourth move. This article pursues a further line of enquiry, one that is implicit rather than explicit in the major topoi of René Girard's analysis. Its focus is the monopolization of violence by the state. To underscore the violence of nation-state instrumentalities, one might have pursued an intermediate range of analytical categories derived from the work of the historical sociologist Charles Tilly. More than any other contemporary theorist,

82

Tilly has attempted to show the pervasive though elusive expressions of collective action, from random protest to coordinated contention to collective violence. Tilly has also underscored the inescapable context for all analyses of collective violence: 'the mapping of the world into mutually exclusive national states', a mapping that has taken place only during 'our own extraordinary era'.[1]

Tilly's analysis, however, is derived from a close reading of the modern history of western Europe, as he himself readily acknowledges. In order to chart some of the distinctive features about violence within a Muslim nation-state context, one must begin where Islam begins, in Africa and Asia.[2] It must also situate Islam in a pattern of global rather than European history. For these reasons, I have chosen to look instead at the theoretical explorations of the British sociologist Anthony Giddens. Giddens makes explicit universalist claims. He surveys a broad range of historical evidence about political theory and practice. And, most importantly, he invokes religion, along with ideology and power, as constructs for understanding the nature of contemporary, global patterns of violence.

There are also limits to Giddens' postulates. I suggest that we can best understand these limits as well as the advances of his work by examining how a putatively Islamic idiom of violence has been forged within one nation-state, the dominant polity of South-East Asia, Indonesia. But first we must make clear what is meant by Islam, especially since Islam is so often and guilelessly invoked as if it were a self-evident, unproblematic category of collective religious identity. It is neither self-evident nor unproblematic. It is as much the locus of contention as Judaism, Christianity, or the very category 'religion'.

The Nation State: Arbiter or Catalyst of Violence?

Noting its absence in most analyses of Islam, Clifford Geertz called for the exercise of negative capability, by which he meant a passion for tact, openness and tolerance when confronting uncertainties, mysteries, doubts.[3] So much has been written about Islam during the past decade that one might have dared to hope that uncertainties had been removed, mysteries lifted, doubts vanished. Alas, stereotypes die hard. None is more durable than the notion that Islam is intrinsically, irretrievably violent. The Quran preaches holy war, and Muslims want to be holy warriors, to die, if necessary, as martyrs to the faith. That common assumption is not true, at least no more true than the equally fatuous notions that Christians must be poor or Jews must be merchants.

Nonetheless, most Americans, together with most Europeans, most of the time link Islam to violence. The reflex that conjoins Islam inextricably with violence prevails. Why?

In part, it prevails because of journalistic license. The best reporters strive to be ambivalent, to give both or many sides of the same story. Journalism, however, remains the companion rather than the pacesetter of mass communication. As long as most readers expect them, reporters and editors will provide headlines that attribute to fundamentalists, extremists, and terrorists Islamic motivations. Even when some Muslims do terrorize in the name of Islam, is that true Islam? It is a simple question. It should be constantly asked. It seldom is, at least in the popular press. Instead, Islam has become the major carrier for those infantile fantasies and magic-like superstitions that were thought to characterize all religions before the coming of light, before the age of science and technology. The demonization of Islam is a long, unpleasant saga. The 1989 chapter pitted an aged and bigoted cleric against an 'innocent', gifted writer. Khomeini is dead, Rushdie in hiding, but the 1990 chapter replaced Khomeini and Rushdie with Saddam Hussein and George Bush, continuing the notion that the crescent reviles, while the cross exalts, universal human values. Such thoughtless reductionisms need to be excised, and in other works I have signalled some ways to begin this long and still hazardous project.[4]

There is another story that can and should be told. *Islam has ceased to be, if it ever fully was, an independent variable in Muslim societies.* The dominant rubric for the social as well as the political domain is the nation state. The nation state not only controls the mechanisms of power it also curtails, without eliminating, the possibility of Islamicly induced violence. Muslims may still fight, kill and die, but they do so, with rare exceptions, as members of nation states or, in the case of Palestinians and Azerbaijanis, as members of umbrella groups struggling to become a nation state.

All Muslim polities are Third World, or to use the Wallersteinian/ Chirot vocabulary, they belong to the periphery rather than the core of sovereign states which determine the major directions of global exchange in the late twentieth century.[5] Richard Falk observed that with reference to the Third World it may be better to speak of state nation than nation state since 'most of the political entities that have emerged in the non-Western world since 1945 . . . have established the formal structure of governance and have acquired sovereign status in internal and external affairs . . . (yet lack) the psychosocial basis of membership – the sense of affiliation that generates pride in nationality and citizenship'.[6]

Even as state nations, however, they aspire to become that which they regard as the minimal model for global recognition: internally pacified, externally projective sovereign entities known as nation states. Muslims are no exception, and to the extent that nation building and demands of citizenship compete with Islamic loyalties, one must weigh their respective force. It is our contention that the battle is uneven, that national identity has created its own variant of entropy, that Islamic legacies, values, and symbols are subsumed within and transformed by a metareligious, global realignment of power.

Stated even more boldly, if we consider only Islam and violence, it would be possible to agree that the headlines are correct, at least some of the time, and that Islam has provided the ideological incentive for violence. But if we expand our range of variables and include the influence of the nation state, the equation of Islam with violence is neither simple nor inevitable. It is the nation state which has implemented violence at a new level, and in so doing, complicated the Islamic factor, even for those committed Muslims who continue to identify Islam as a holistic worldview with durative impact on their lives.

Anthony Giddens has written the most challenging book on the interface of the nation state and violence. In volume 2 of his announced trilogy, *A Contemporary Critique of Historical Materialism*, he opposes Marx and Marxists, neo-Marxists and post-Marxists in offering a revisionist view of the emergence of the modern world. The crucial demarcations for Giddens occurred in the transition from traditional polities to absolutist empires to modern nation states. While capitalistic enterprise and industrial production assisted the emergence of the nation state, equally determinative in his view were heightened surveillance and 'the consolidation of centralized control of the means of violence'.

Just as violence is paired with nation state in the title of Giddens' book, so the concept of violence looms large throughout his heavily freighted argument. It is, for instance, the linchpin in defining the nation state as 'a set of institutional forms of governance maintaining an administrative monopoly over a territory with demarcated boundaries [borders], its rule being sanctioned by law and direct control of the means of internal and external violence'.[7]

Giddens' approach cannot be commended for its definitional consistency. Distancing himself from Bourdieu and other continental theorists, he claims that what he means by 'control of the means of violence' is 'control over the capabilities of doing physical harm to the human body through the use of force'.[8] Yet elsewhere he declares that he does not mean merely doing physical harm to others but 'the means of violence associated with the activities of armed forces'.[9] It is in the modern-day nation state that the capability of armed forces has been increased far beyond the war-making potential of their predecessors, the absolutist empires of Europe and Asia. And to Giddens' credit he demonstrates repeatedly how 'the formation of a heightened bureaucratic centralism' leads to a 'a new type of reflexively monitored state system'.[10] So technologically advanced and synchronized have global communications systems become that it is now possible to regularize internal pacification. The nation state, with a monopoly on communications as well as war-making potential, is far more effective at pacifying potential dissidents within its borders than were its absolutist, pre-modern predecessors.

Giddens constantly tries to maintain a dialectical tension within his argument, granting equal time to the analysis of violence on both fronts – internal as well as external. Initially the external front dominates, since its destructive potential is global, if not inter-planetary. One could even read Giddens' entire thesis as an argument on behalf of nuclear comity: so horrific is the prospect of warfare involving nuclear armaments that for over 45 years since Hiroshima and Nagasaki the 'bomb' has never again been exploded, except in test situations. Yet its threatened use persists. The rules of international conflict dictate that further technological refinement of nuclear weaponry will continue apace, as also the temptation to use the 'bomb' at what is perceived to be a crisis moment. The only alternative, in Giddens' view, is to implement a normative political theory of the means of violence, that is, 'the creation of a social order in which use of military power will no longer threaten our existence as a whole'.[11]

This alternative is rankly Utopian. During the explosion of high-tech savagery that has marked the 1991 Gulf War, it seems blithely naive. It is at the least incalculable. For in the interim preceding a nuclear holocaust, all-powerful nation states will continue to claim sovereignty for themselves while vying with others for global resources and prestige. Nation statism is as inevitable as the 'bomb'; no polity can be exempt from its influence. Though Giddens claims to be speaking only of the Western or European nation state,[12] he is also sketching trans-national trends which bear on peripheral polities, including Third World, Muslim nation states. Like Falk, he considers these nation states to be 'in a significant sense state-nations', and like Falk, he uses an internal rather than the external gradient to distinguish them from their more powerful rivals: they have not effected administrative co-ordination to the degree that more industrialized societies have.[13] Yet the political elites of each state-nation do co-opt ideological resources as well as military weaponry, above all in the capital city but also in related urban bureaucratic centers. Policing power expands, 'made possible by the establishment of locales in which the regularized observation of activities [ideological as well as economic] can be carried on in order to seek to control them'.[14]

Ideology is a recurrent concern of *The Nation-State and Violence*. Though bifurcated in the pre-modern state, between the ideology of ruling elites and the ideology of the masses, officialdom within each state, from the ruler down, can promote longevity by imposing a self-serving ideology on all levels of society. One component of ideology may be rationalized religion of the sort depicted by Max Weber. It is the sort of religion in which symbols and rituals, scriptural texts and routinized custodians generate economic profit, or enhance social prestige, or gain military victory or merely under-gird political legitimation – all in the name of God. In short, religion is as susceptible to manipulation as any other ideological resource, once it has been charted in the public rather than the private sphere. It becomes the sum total of its consequences, behavioral patterns writ large. Can religion ever be more? Giddens seems to suggest that in some instances religion may, with difficulty, escape the iron cage of ideology. 'Religion', he allows, 'is not simply ideology – a cloak for asymmetrical domination – but stands in complex relation to the distribution of power'.[15]

Despite that broad disclaimer, Giddens relates religion solely to power, never once elaborating what is the surfeit of meaning or the residue of influence that devolves to religion beyond power in the public sphere.

Chiefly Giddens, like the majority of political theorists, is concerned with the discursive articulation and social consequence of belief systems. In this he is making a thoroughly modernist move, to subsume religion within ideology, to understand it as but one of several reflexes of power. Since violence is a construct of public behavior, it cannot be ratcheted with the sources of religious belief; it can never be understood as something which religion – or more precisely devotees of a particular religion – may internalize on behalf of deeply held, private convictions (for example, Yom Kippur in Judaism, the Crucifixion in Christianity, the martyrdom of Husain in Shii Islam). The nation state dominates public space. It pre-empts violence for its own ends. Violence is legitimated as an extension of the ruling elites' ravenous quest for conformity. Violence becomes the means of enforcing law and order, of preserving the rights of the majority against the tyranny of the minority. It cannot be invoked, its use is not justified on the part of those who act either outside of or against the nation state.

Giddens' approach to violence has protean implications for our assessment of what might be labeled an Islamic idiom of violence. He accents change, privileging discontinuity over structurally antipodal.

There is a chasm – at once unexpected and unbridgeable – between the pre-modern and modern phases of socio-political history. While several factors have contributed to this chasm, four are decisively interrelated in the nation state: extensive, protracted, and systematized surveillance; capitalistic enterprise at all levels; industrial production linked to state goals;[16] and, above all, centralized appropriation of the means of violence. Sharing similar qualities and aspirations, modern nation states can exercise internal control or pacification with far more powerful instrumentalities than their predecessors. Collectively they dissolve the boundary between government and society. Modern societies are defined by that organizational rubric which they commonly share: they are all 'nation-states, existing within a nation-state system'.[17]

As the power of the center has continued to magnify, the ideological options available within each polity can no longer escape relatedness to the center. Sub-groups, whether tribal or regional, factional or sectarian, must respond to centripetal pressures: they are either co-opted for the goals of the ruling elites or coerced to comply with the dominant ideology, even when that ideology is offensive to long-standing traditions that they cherish.

Applied to Muslim societies, Giddens' analysis has two immediate implications that signal a shift from most of the popular commentary that claims explanatory force, whether in journalistic writing or in academic research that is subtly driven by journalistic priorities. *First, the state is always prioritized over society. No sub-group can act either spontaneously or independent of the center*. Citizenship is above all defined through the nation state and the mass army that supports and extends its dictates.[18] Even so-called religious revivalism depends on manipulation from above rather than social/class cleavages or psychological reflexes of anomie. In the case of Islam, the parameters of revivalism are monitored by state functionaries, their dissent curbed through state intervention. Security forces are at once powerful and pervasive. 'Militant Islam' is never autonomous: it is held hostage to a religious ideology that expresses specific group interests, whether shaped at the center by pragmatic elites or instigated on the periphery by zealous believers. An Islam so malleable is not the property of only one group nor may it be pressed into service for a single, consensual goal.[19]

Second, Islam is a dependent as well as an independent variable in the construction of nation state interests. Internal cohesion, regional prowess, international accessibility – all are aspects of the new world-system that has emerged only in the twentieth century, in large part due to the demands of the world capitalist economy. To speak of Islam as though it operated outside of or independent of this system and its strictures is to ignore the level of change that pervades the contemporary era. Rhetorical strategies may invoke an independent role for Islamic values, even as they conjure up a revered past of Islamic successes, but the structural restraints of modernity impose on Islam – as on Christianity and Judaism, Buddhism and Hinduism, Confucianism and Shinto – a subordinate role in each nation state.

The Case of Indonesia – Eccentric or Normative?

One could trace the implications of this process in any number of Muslim nation states. I have selected Indonesia precisely because it is so jarring to most perceptions of Islam and Islamicly-coded violence. Indonesia will never rival Middle Eastern or South Asian or North African Muslim polities for those who create the headlines of Euro-America. No matter how often one stresses the size and importance of South-East Asian Islam, it is Vietnam not Islam that encapsulates the popular view of the world's largest archipelago.

Despite the force of common wisdom, I would argue that few Muslim nation states have inspired such conflicting estimates of what Islamic identity or Islamic loyalty might mean as does Indonesia. Islam was introduced into this Pacific sub-region gradually over centuries through foreign traders of both Indian and Arab origin. Did Islam cease to be an external force, becoming instead transformed by the Indonesian environment – at once tropical and accommodationist? This has been the view of numerous scholars, including Clifford Geertz in his two best known books on the subject, *The Religion of Java* (1960) and *Islam Observed* (1971). It is a view that has also been echoed by more recent analysts, notably Benedict R. O'G. Anderson[20] and Ruth McVey.[21]

The opposite stance has also had its defenders: Islam never ceased to be foreign, always presenting another worldview, at once universalizing and proselytizing. Islam by its nature must transform every society and culture once the Quran has been announced, the Prophet embraced and the Sharia or Islamic law implemented. This has been the view of the only bona fide Indonesian revivalist movement, the Muhammadijah,[22] and also outspoken Muslim politicians such as Mohammad Natsir and Abdurrachman Wahid.

Nor can the question of 'true' Islam be answered with reference to statistics. Even the best statistics can be misleading, open, as they are, to multiple interpretations. On paper Indonesia is the largest Muslim country in the world; it numbers over 140 million Muslims among its 165 million inhabitants. The next closest country is either India, Pakistan, or Bangladesh, depending on whose census figures you believe, but the

Muslim population which each boasts does not exceed 90–100 million. Indonesia has no competition if one's sole preoccupation is to count Muslim noses.

Yet Indonesia is also a series of islands dominated by one island, Java. Less than seven per cent of Indonesia's total land mass, Java contains more than half its total population. Politically and economically it accounts for much more than half: Javanese ruling elites will settle for nothing less than domination of the entire archipelago. Recent history is on their side. The Javanese were the major power-brokers in Jakarta before it ever became the capital of a newly-consolidated nation state after World War II. Dutch rule was introduced in the seventeenth century. Faced with major indigenous uprisings in the nineteenth century, the Dutch won because they combined superior firepower with adroit manipulation of divisions among Javanese Muslims. In both the decisive Java War (1826–30) and the protracted Aceh War (1873–1910) the Dutch courted Muslim sub-groups as their allies in fighting other Muslim subgroups. Dutch colonial rule persisted; the 'Muslims' lost.

Java then as now held the key to power. By geography it is crucial to commercial and communication networks that link the islands farther east to the outside world. It is a highly stratified society, with bureaucratic elites holding the purse-strings of wealth and at the same time controlling the arsenals of military/political power. Nominally Muslims, upper-class Javanese are beholden neither to the ulama nor to reformist platforms of Islamic loyalty. As one joke has it, the Javanese are Christlams who eat four-legged chickens (pork). That is a semeiotic statement about their mentors. They are Christlams because they have internalized Dutch values even while projecting an Islamic identity. At the same time, their dietary laxity conforms with the preferences of their neighbors to the north, the Chinese. It is a laxity daily abetted by the example of the prosperous three to four million Indonesians of Chinese descent, most of whom reside on Java.

In view of the stark features of Javanese hegemony, it is remarkable that anyone could have imagined that Indonesia might become an intensely cohesive religious state, an Islamic polity of the Indian Ocean. One observer, the itinerant journalist Godfrey Jansen, did rush to make just that judgment. Soon after the 1979 debacle in Iran, he predicted that Indonesia would be the next country to witness an Islamic revolution.[23] We are still waiting and we will wait a long time before such an upheaval overtakes either Jakarta or the Javanese patrimonial elites who continue to support General T.N.J. Suharto, as they did his predecessor President Achmed Sukarno.

Most political histories stress that the shift from Sukarno to Suharto introduced a major fault-line into modern, post-independence Indonesia. In 1965, following what was alleged to be a communist-inspired uprising against the central government, Suharto came to power. His mission, he proclaimed, was to institute the New Order. From an Islamic viewpoint, the New Order has had even less relationship to Quranic values than did the Old Order. In 1973, for instance, Suharto combined the four Muslim political parties into one and refused to allow an Islamic word in the new name of the amalgated party. To avoid an overtly anti-Islamic message the move was embellished with a veneer of consistency: five minority non-Muslim parties were also merged into a single party at the same time. Hence, as one observer has astutely noted, 'apart from Golkar [the government party], only [two other parties,] the [Muslim] PPP and [the non-Muslim] PDI remained. At a single stroke, the number of parties competing for votes at elections was reduced to three and religion ceased to define any political party ideology'.[24]

Though publicly erased, Islamicly-mobilized politicians retained an activist edge due to the clamor surrounding the proposed change in marriage laws in 1973. Some, such as the tiny splinter group called the Terror Warman group, went underground (between 1978 and 1981).[25] The next stage of overt struggle was provoked with the introduction of the Social Organizations Bill of 1983–84. In its aftermath occurred the only wide-scale Islamicly-related disturbance to rock Indonesia during Suharto's tenure. Since nearly every commentator cites it as 'clear' evidence of Islamic unrest, portending a future upsurge in the purchase of Islamic values among Indonesians as a whole, it bears closer examination.

The disturbance is known euphemistically as the Tanjung Priok incident. It is named after the dock facilities sub-district of Jakarta port. Economically depressed in the best of times, the area was hit especially hard by the reduction of goods shipped through Jakarta during the world recession of the early 1980s. The dock workers, many of them unemployed, were wont to protest what they saw as arbitrary government policies that ignored their plight and neglected their needs. A protest poster was hung in a local prayer compound. Two local constables removed it without, however, removing their shoes. They also sprayed gutter water on the prayer-wall where the offensive poster had been hung. Mosque officials protested this breach of etiquette to the local military district. Two days later, while trying to resolve their dispute with the authorities, some bystanders set fire to an officer's motorcycle. District headquarters immediately dispatched other officers to arrest the arsonists. Along with them four representatives of the prayer compound were also arrested 'by mistake'. Other Tanjung Priok residents affiliated with the prayer compound next tried to secure the release of the detainees. When they failed, they organized a peaceful protest march on the district headquarters.

It was during this march, on 12 September 1984, that the incident reached its ugly climax: about 1,500 marchers were met 'by a number of armored vehicles and fully armed troops who got off several trucks'. Fired upon, the marchers fled in all directions. 'Approximately 60 local people were shot dead and over 100 wounded. It seems that there were no casualties among the soldiers.'[26]

Some were quick to draw from the incident a portent of large-scale urban discontent. 'A process of polarization had begun which would not stop until the opportunity to participate in politics became available for many more groups in Indonesian society.'[27]

An opposite view was also possible. As mentioned above, the Suharto regime had proposed the Social Organizations Bill during 1983–84. It was intended to clarify Pancasila as the sole ideological foundation of Indonesian society. Prior to being implemented in 1985, it had been approved by both the PPP and Golkar. The Tanjung Priok incident occurred right after the draft law had been submitted to parliament and before it had gained final ratification. Suharto feared a Muslim political backlash. Following the 1965 liquidation of the communist menace, Islamic values as embodied in schools, mosques and their affiliates had been touted as the regime's principal ideological adversary. By 1983 the assertion of Pancasila as *asas tunggal* (sole ideology) had become an essential tactical priority. Is it surprising then that lawyers defending Muslim activists later sought to show that the demonstration was itself a staged provocation? Its timing could not have better suited the regime's political agenda. By intimidating Muslim activists, Suharto underscored the message that any protest against the state would be interpreted as dissent from the *asas tunggal* requirement. The real message of Tanjung Priok was not that Muslim activism was on the rise but that any 'loud' peep of Muslim protest would be muffled with overwhelming, brute force.

The sequel to the Tanjung Priok incident favors the latter interpretation. No action was taken to remedy the harm caused by police malfeasance. Ignored was the white paper drafted within a week after the massacre and signed by the Petition-of-50 opposition group; it accused the government of failing to live up to the ideals of Pancasila! Instead, the commander of the Indonesian armed forces painted the protest as a subversive activity put down by patriotic officers. Moreover, he claimed that only nine persons had been killed. When two Indonesian Muslim youth organizations tried to resist the Societies Law after its passage, they were summarily brought into line, one agreeing to comply with its dicta, the other withdrawing from political activities altogether.

The most significant action, however, was the attempt to reconstruct Indonesian history in the aftermath of the Tanjung Priok incident. In November 1987 General Suharto, together with Commander-in-Chief Benny Murdani, opened a new museum. It was devoted to glorifying the role and exploits of the Indonesian Army as custodians of 'Pancasila Islam' in its battles against Muslim rebels and opponents. In exhibit after exhibit 'it tells the story of the army's crackdown on dissident Muslims following the slaughter of dozens of innocent demonstrators in Tanjung Priok in September 1984'.[28]

All the details of the Tanjung Priok incident underscore what could be gleaned from a reading of Giddens and an extrapolation of his analysis to the Islamic world in general and Indonesia in particular. The nation state has extraordinary power to monitor reflexively all activities within its borders. The state can achieve internal pacification, even when dissidents still appear to have an independent voice.

The debate over Pancasila more than anything else indicates how ethereal are the hopes of injecting an Islamic mandate into the political profile of late twentieth century Indonesia. It is naive to continue to speak about a gap between Muslims and the government, as if the Javanese ruling elites had somehow permitted themselves to be caught on such an ideological whip-saw.[29] The opposite situation prevails: the government does not have to find a *rapprochement* with Muslims because it has learned from Sukarno, and before him the Dutch, how to successfully infiltrate and diffuse oppositional groups.

Consider the PPP. It became a new umbrella group of Muslim political parties when the state refused to allow the Muslim modernist party, Masjumi, banned in 1965, to reorganize under its old name. In 1968 it became Parmusi and then in 1973 it was forcibly combined with other Muslim parties, including the traditionalist Nahdatal Ulema (NU) into a new federation known as Partai Persatuan Pembangunan, or PPP (United Development Party). The PPP did well enough in the 1977 elections to win a third of the parliamentary seats that it contested, yet patronage from the center, in the form of positions and munificences awarded by Suharto, strengthened pro-regime leaders and fostered their rise within PPP. Though PPP had never been free of factionalism, the dominant group, both numerically and ideologically, from 1973 to the early 1980s had been the NU. It embodied the residue of traditional Islamic loyalties. To subvert these loyalties Suharto hand-picked a crafty operative, Johnny Naro. Approaching the 1982 elections Naro manipulated the candidate lists in such a manner that he excluded NU 'troublemakers'. In other words, the most aggressive Islamic candidates were not allowed to stand for election. How did they protest their exclusion? The largest faction of NU withdrew from the PPP and foreswore all active engagement in politics. As a result, by August 1984 Johnny Naro had become the undisputed leader of PPP; it is a position he continues to hold.[30]

But Muslim dissidents knew full well what Johnny Naro represented and how he came to a position of political power. Deprived of even a parliamentary option to register their grievances, many spoke out in the aftermath of the Tanjung Priok incident; it was, after all, their sole avenue for protest. The government reacted by treating their protest as tantamount to treason: seizing suspects without warrants, Indonesian security police arrested scores of Muslims, many of whom, like A. M. Fatwa (see below), had little or no connection with the actual Tanjung Priok march.

Some Tentative Conclusions

In the aftermath of the coming to power of the Islamic Republic of Iran, Michael Fischer asked the astute question: 'Is it possible to have a revolution in the traditional sense in the late twentieth century?'[31] For those who expect a transformation of the nation state to reflect any other agenda than maintenance of power and competition with rival nation states through rational, secular, and technological instrumentalities the answer is *no*. It is the same answer for the handful of dissidents who still hope for an Islamic alternative in Indonesia as it is for the clergy who continue to administer from Tehran since Khomeini's demise. Ideology may be invoked but pragmatism succeeds, and violence has become the exclusive, if unadmitted, property of the nation state.

The Indonesian difference is that no Islamic group enjoys enough popular support to mount a sustained challenge to the Suharto regime. In 1978 James Peacock shrewdly observed about the Muhammadijah that they had 'not converted the value system of the entire Indonesian nation . . . but [instead] remained one of several important value systems'.[32] In 1991 the question is whether or not reformist Islam even remains an 'important' value system. To be important it must be discrete, it must be able to project an autonomous viewpoint to outsiders. But can it? Government censorship monitors all print and television reports within the archipelago, and subtly it may also shape the image of Indonesian Islamic dissidents that is projected abroad.

Coverage of the Tanjung Priok incident, far from lauding the role of independent Muslim activists, reveals the extent to which overseas journalistic media – not only newspapers but also monthly and quarterly periodicals – have been pressed into the service of the media control branch of the Jakarta bureaucracy. A case in point is the periodical *Inside Indonesia*. Based in Australia, it attempts to give genuine voice to oppositional elements within the Javanese-dominated nationalist administration. In a nine-page feature article its editors made clear that, in their opinion, the government had manipulated the Tanjung Priok incident to its own benefit. The final essay featured the personality profile of a leading Javanese Muslim dissident. His name was A. M. Fatwa. Though opposed to the government's manipulation of Pancasila, he had demurred from participating in the Tanjung Priok protest march. He was still arrested. Why? Because he had met with one of the signatories to the white paper petition criticizing the brutal military action. The action was as unjust as it was arbitrary, yet its reportage, like the article as a whole, does little more than evoke a mood of frustration among Muslim activists; it provides no analysis of why these individuals were held on such a short leash by the Suharto regime.

By contrast, the Marxist *Journal of Contemporary Asia* painted a very broad picture of international intrigue and diplomatic maneuvering. It linked all of South-East Asia to major Middle Eastern players. The article was even titled 'Radical Islam in Southeast Asia: Rhetoric and Reality in the Middle Eastern Connection'. Its author made only brief mention of what he labeled the Tanjung Priok uprising. Yet he went on to note that in its aftermath 'Jakarta and other centres in East and central Java were flooded with pamphlets exhorting the faithful to defend Islam by arms'.[33] Such pamphlets may or may not have inspired subsequent bomb explosions in Jakarta and Bandung and the dynamiting of part of the Borobodor temple complex, a major Buddhish symbol of pre-Muslim Indonesia. It was these latter actions, never mentioned by *Inside Indonesia*, which provided the immediate pretext for the government to round up numerous Muslim activists and have them arrested as suspects.

The Iranian embassay in Jakarta had hoped for more. The Iranians, observes the author, had speculated that the Suharto regime would over-react and then experience a fate similar to that of the Shah: it would be toppled by an Islamicly-motivated upheaval. When the only detonations after Tanjung Priok were directed at buildings rather than people, Iranian realists concluded that the New Order regime of General Suharto had won an ideological victory. Had it not convinced would-be Muslim activists that it was 'even more prepared [than was President

Sukarno] to impose Pancasila as a political, ideological and national philosophy at any cost?'[34]

The article voids further commentary. It is content to record failed conspiracies. It does not place the sequence of events surrounding Tanjung Priok into a holistic perspective, relating them to a pattern of oppression that characterized both Sukarno's Old Order and Suharto's New Order.

Strangely, that task is left to an indigenous Indonesian businessman of Chinese origin, Liem Soei Liong. In an expose unmatched for its detailed analysis, Liem indicates how the Indonesian Army had been doctrinated even before 1965 to regard all its enemies as advocates of either left-wing or right-wing extremism. Left-wing extremists were the communists, who had been curbed in 1949 and then all but exterminated in 1965. 'Right-wing extremism was automatically identified with Muslim political forces', going back to the Darul Islam revolts that erupted in the 1950s. 'This constant exposure to Darul Islam on the battlefield only served to harden the attitudes of the Indonesian military towards the organized political Islamic opposition.'[35]

Seen in this light, the Tanjung Priok incident becomes a convenient stepping-stone in the military's strategy to eliminate the Islamic opposition. During the remainder of 1984 it was Muslim preacher/activists who were arrested in droves. Could it be that the same pattern of incarceration and brutalization which had been applied to communists after 1965 was now being applied to Muslim dissidents? In the opinion of the author, yes – and it succeeded. So grim is the fate of such prisoners and so common knowledge is their fate that open-air rallies to listen to popular, free-speaking preachers abruptly ceased. Instead much smaller groups gathered informally inside houses. But even these meetings were deemed to be a menace to the regime, and by 1986 the Javanese military authorites had labeled them as 'communist-style organizations'. They were repressed with heavy-handed tactics.

All the available options for Indonesian Muslim activists were foreclosed. The author has described how it is that they gradually came to be foreclosed. What political future could there be for ardent Muslims in Suharto's Indonesia? None, it would seem. Yet in the very last sentence, Liem Soei Liong declares: 'If one assumes that repression of political expression can be likened to a cap being held on an active volcano, sooner or later there will be an explosion; only the Muslims seem to be more or less preparing themselves for a new dawn in Indonesia'.[36]

That conclusion would be astonishing, not to mention illogical, if it did not have a sub-text to explain the author's abrupt volte-face. The subtext becomes evident when one realizes the full identity of Liem Soei Liong.

Not only is he an Indonesian businessman of Chinese origin, but he is by all accounts Indonesia's richest man! According to *Inside Indonesia*, he is a business partner to the Suharto family (which would explain the continuation, if not the source, of his wealth).[37] The *Journal of Contemporary Asia* is even more direct: Liem Soei Liong is 'the most notorious *cukong* (capitalist crony) partner of Suharto'.[38] Could any one without these connections have been allowed to accumulate such detailed information about the government's Islamic policy? No, and yet to conceal these same connections it must disavow the soundness of his own analysis by throwing a sop to Islamists at the end of his extraordinary article.

Another discrete datum provides an explanation for the author's blithe deference to Islamic triumphalism: among the bombings that occurred after the Tanjung Priok slaughter were three time-bombs placed in branches of the Central Asia Bank. Who owns the Central Asia Bank? Liem Soei Liong. By addressing the issue of Indonesian Muslim activism in an international forum (the *Third World Quarterly* is published from London by a Pakistani expatriate, Altaf Gauhar), Liem Soei Liong could demonstrate his concern for Islamic causes. A Pancasila pluralist would be pleased by his several arguments for the failure of Muslim political dissidents, as Suharto and his other cronies undoubtedly were, but after having demonstrated why Muslim activists will fail in the near future, Liem can also predict their long-term success . . . without risk to his business associates. Even were his prediction to do no more than cause some activists to hesitate before planting another bomb in one of his banks, he would have won a double victory.[39]

His prediction, of course, could still be wrong. A coalition of fearless Muslim intellectuals and masses, disenchanted with a toothless version of Pancasila, might co-ordinate an Islamic takeover of the Javanese capital in the near future. Yet even if they did, their victory would not bring success for their cause. After confounding both Liem Soei Liong and Javanese patrimonial elites, they would still be caught in the same game of strategizing on behalf of political interests. Despite initial misgivings, they would be forced to resort to the same instrumentalities, ideological as well as military, of the modern nation state in order to accomplish their goals. Giddens' message, while unsavory, is alas correct: there are no alternatives to the nation state than those which it provides, and violence as well as victory, the international as well as the domestic press, are on its side. Dissidents, including Islamicly-motivated activists, may try to co-opt but they can never transform the state. It is integral to a world-system with powerful capitalist stimuli and insatiable autocratic brokers. Islam is not an autonomous but a subordinate system; truly Islamic violence has been rendered mute.

Yet the interpretation of violence within an Islamic frame of reference remains open to further gambits. The political theory of Giddens, while it helps to demonstrate the pervasiveness of centrist structures within Islamdom as well as Christendom, does not finally exhaust the appeals of religious rhetoric or the uses of religious ritual. The ideological forum may be the most evident playing field of power, politics, and the press yet mythomoteurs take shape within the hearts and minds of men and women beyond the public gaze. Literary markings of myth yield insight through critical forays of the kind that René Girard has so skilfully charted, and it remains an important task for those who know subaltern groups within Indonesia, as also their textual legacy, be it oral or written, to apply Girardian analyses to the same dilemma of Islamic violence surveyed in this article. The analysis of violence, like violence itself, has not been played out; it has merely begun a new and formidable phase of its hydra-headed existence.

NOTES

1. Charles Tilly, Louise Tilly, and Richard Tilly, *The Rebellious Century 1830–1930* (Cambridge, MA: Harvard University Press, 1975), p.291. For other elaborations of his wideranging enquiry into violence, see Charles Tilly, *The Contentious French* (Cambridge, MA: Harvard University Press, 1986), and also Lynn Hunt, 'Charles Tilly's Collective Action' in Theda Skoopol (ed.), *Vision and Method in Historical Sociology* (Cambridge: Cambridge University Press, 1984), pp.244–75.
2. I subsume the Middle East within Asia, since properly speaking it is West Asia, the alternative, and popular, term Middle East having been introduced by the British to depict a part of their colonial empire.
3. Clifford Geertz, 'Conjuring with Islam', *New York Review of Books*, 27 May 1982: p.25.
4. See *Defenders of God: The Fundamentalist Revolt against the Modern Age* (San Francisco, CA: Harper San Francisco, 1989), Ch. 8 and conclusion; also, 'Holy war (jihad) in Islamic Religion and Nation-state Ideologies', forthcoming in John Kelsay and James Turner Johnson (eds.), *War, Peace, and Statecraft in Islam and Christianity* (Westport, CT: Greenwood Press, 1991).
5. Daniel Chirot in *Social Change in the Modern Era* (Orlando, FL: Harcourt Brace Jovanovich, 1986) modifies the core-periphery distinction first elaborated by Wallerstein. See also Charles Ragin and Daniel Chirot, 'The World System of Immanuel Wallerstein: Sociology and Politics as History' in Theda Skoopol (ed.), *Vision and Method in Historical Sociology* (New York, NY: Cambridge University Press, 1904), pp.276–312.
6. Richard A. Falk, *This Endangered Planet: Prospects and Proposals for Human Survival* (New York, NY: Vintage Books, 1972), pp.223–24.
7. Anthony Giddens, *The Nation-State and Violence: Volume Two of a Contemporary Critique of Historical Materialism* (Berkeley, CA: University of California Press, 1987), p.121.
8. Ibid., p.343, Ch. 1, note 20.

9. Ibid., p.121.
10. Ibid., p.103.
11. Ibid., p.329.
12. Ibid., p.5.
13. Ibid., p.252.
14. Ibid., p.186. Giddens relates this surveillance or monitoring function chiefly to production and the work-place, yet it applies equally well to the activities of cultural dissidents, i.e., those who embrace religious or ideological positions at variance with the center.
15. Ibid, p.74.
16. Capitalistic enterprise and industrial production must, of course, be differentiated on a global pattern. Summarily, they may be described as coordinate to the state in the First World, regulated by the state in the Second World while still embryonic in most of the Third World. The distinctions are wholesale, and also subject to the caveat of ambiguity that afflicts any aggregative topoi; see, for instance, Carl E. Pletsch, 'The Three Worlds, or the Division of Social Scientific Labor, circa 1950–1975', Comparative Studies in Society and History, Vol. 23, No. 4 (Oct. 1981), pp.565–90.
17. Giddens, op. cit., p.1.
18. In Giddens' words, 'the nation-state and the mass army appear together, the twin tokens of citizenship within territorially bordered political communities', p.233.
19. Understating the centripetal power of the nation-state is the great weakness of Reinhold Loeffler's otherwise remarkable book, Islam in Practice: Religious Belief in a Persian Village (Albany, NY: SUNY Press, 1988). While it is a healthy corrective to the notion that everyone in Iran accepts the mythology of rule deriving from a clerical theocracy, it is based on interviews with less than one hundred individuals in a large tribal village (whose total population is perhaps 3,000). Such a data base is too small to be representative: Iran boasts almost 50 million inhabitants, 75 per cent of whom live in urban or semi-urban environments! And post-1979 it is instrumentalities of the nation state which continue to shape opinions and curtail responses beyond the center. Although illiterate as well as literate Iranians may criticize the government through the ballot box, 'the arrival of public telephone and television has ensured the regime's hold over the rural areas. Every Friday the village clergyman will tell the villagers more or less what Rafsanjani has told the Tehranis in person, interpreting the latest shift in the political situation with regard to war and peace, foreign policy, economy and religious issues'. Baqir Moin, 'Iran and Islam' in Marvin Wright, (ed.) Iran: The Khomeini Revolution (London: Longman, 1989) p.76.
20. Benedict R. O'G. Anderson, 'The Idea of Power in Javanese Culture' in Claire Holt (ed.), Culture and Power in Indonesia (Ithaca, NY: Cornell University Press, 1972), pp.1–69 but especially pp.57–62.
21. Ruth McVey, 'Faith as the Outsider: Islam in Indonesia' in James Piscatori (ed.), Islam in the Political Process (New York NY: Cambridge University Press, 1983), pp.199–225.
22. On the Muhammadijah, see the still unsurpassed studies of James L. Peacock, Muslim Puritans: Reformist Psychology in Southeast Asian Islam (Berkeley, CA and London: University of California Press, 1978) and Purifying the Faith: The Muhammadijah Movement in Indonesian Islam (Menlo Park, CA: Benjamin/Cummings Publishing Company, 1978).
23. G. H. Jansen, Militant Islam (London and Sydney: Pan Books, 1979), p.198.
24. A. D. Johns. 'Indonesia: Islam and Cultural Pluralism' in John Esposito (ed.), Islam in Asia: Religion, Politics and Society (New York, NY: Oxford University Press, 1987), p.217.
25. For references to the Terror Warman group and also to the articles on Indonesian Islam in both Inside Indonesia and the Journal of Contemporary Asia, I am indebted to June Santosa, a graduate student in Islamic studies and sociology at Boston University.

26. The details of this account, as also both quotations, come from Max Lane, 'The Tanjung Priok Incident: Simmering Discontent Bubbles Over' in *Inside Indonesia* (Bulletin of the Indonesia Resources and Information Programme [IRIP]) No. 4, (March 1985) pp.1–9.
27. Ibid., p.8.
28. Liem Soei Liong, 'Indonesian Muslims and the State: Accommodation or Revolt?', *Third World Quarterly*, Vol. 10, No. 2 (April 1988), p.877.
29. Deliar Noer, 'Contemporary Political Dimensions of Islam' in M.B. Hooker (ed.), *Islam in South-East Asia* (Leiden: E.J.Brill, 1983), p.198.
30. Liem, op. cit., p.886.
31. Michael Fischer, 'Repetitions in the Iranian Revolution' in Martin Kramer (ed.), *Shiism, Resistance and Revolution* (Boulder, CO: Westview Press, 1987), p.131.
32. Peacock, *Purifying the Faith*, p.106.
33. Geoffrey C. Gunn, 'Radical Islam in Southeast Asia', *Journal of Contemporary Asia*, Vol. 16, No. 1 (1986), p.44.
34. Ibid.: p.45. The emphases are mine.
35. Liem, op. cit., p.877.
36. Ibid., p.896.
37. Lane, op. cit., p.8.
38. Gunn, op. cit., p.44.
39. His gamble appears to have succeeded, at least for now. The *Muslim World Book Review* (*MWBR*) is an unabashedly partisan quarterly edited by and for overseas Muslim activists. In *MWBR* Vol. 10, No. 1 (Autumn 1989): p.49, Liem's article is singled out for praise, the reviewer noting with approval his critique of Pancasila!
   No allusion is made either to Liem's ambivalence about Islam or to the likely source of his abundant details about the Islamic opposition to Suharto.

Sacrifice and Cosmic War

MARK JUERGENSMEYER

A small design at the center of the cover of the paperback edition of René Girard's impressive *Violence and the Sacred* admirably states the theme.[1] There, in blood red, is the silhouette of a kneeling, bound human victim, his head on a chopping block. Above him stands the priestly figure, holding a menacing axe suspended in air in the final horrible moment before it falls and strikes its unhappy target. As the cover suggests, sacrifice is indeed at the heart of Girard's reflections on the relation of religion and violence – and human sacrifice at that. For in Girard's way of thinking, the idea of sacrifice is linked with the impulse of humans to destroy one another, even when this savage desire is symbolically deflected towards a scapegoat foe. What the ritual of sacrifice does, according to Girard, is to allow the impulse to be vented symbolically with relatively little bloodshed. This aspect of Girard's thought is also captured in the cover's design: the artist's axe, frozen in time, never actually falls.

Yet in recent years religious axes seem to be falling everywhere. For this reason, although it is easy to assent to the first premise of Girard's thesis – that sacrifice is an important and frequent characteristic of religious imagination – it remains open to question whether sacrificial rites and symbols discourage violence in the real world, including the sort of religious terrorism that we have seen so much of in the past decade. Is this terrorism due only to the failure of religious ritual to function correctly, creating what Girard calls a 'sacrificial crisis'? Or, when ritual swells 'the surging tide of impure violence instead of channelling it', as Girard puts it,[2] is it due to something else, perhaps a tendency towards violence more endemic to religion than Girard's theories would admit?

In this essay I want to reflect on these questions. Although enormously indebted to Girard for stimulating my thinking about these matters, I will look for a strand of logic somewhat different from the one proposed by Girard to comprehend the role of sacrifice in religious thought and to discern the connection between symbolic violence and violence that is actually aimed at harming another person. The difference between my approach and Girard's is partly a matter of our starting points. My interest in the topic has come from analyses of contemporary acts of violence rather than textual images of them. The ideas with which I have worked emerged from my research on militant Sikhs in India, Sinhalese Buddhist activists in Sri Lanka, and other present-day religious revolutionaries around the world.[3] I found in all of these cases that religious language is combined with specific attempts to impose perceptions of order on disorder. Those who attempt to impose their notion of order feel that there is a basic conflict between the two, and the battle between order and disorder is ultimately waged on a cosmic plane. It is this grand struggle, sometimes mythic and sometimes meta-physical, that seems to lie only slightly beneath the real engagements of religious activists, and that often connects their acts with what Girard rightly identifies as that other, safer, form of religious violence: the sacrificial event.

The Centrality of Sacrifice

The altar – symbol of a sacred chopping block – and the priest, originally a sacred executioner, remain today at the focal point of worship throughout the world in a surprising variety of religious contexts. They, and the notions of sacrifice and martyrdom that lie behind them, are so integral to religion that without them many religious concepts would be almost unthinkable.

One finds sacrificial acts at the center of some of the most ancient religious traditions. Many of the Vedic texts of Hinduism, which are at least 2,500 years old, seem to be formulae for performing animal sacrifices. The Vedic Agnicayana ritual – some 3,000 years old and arguably the world's oldest ritual still being performed – involves the elaborate construction of a sacrifical altar on which is made an offering. Today the offering is *ghi*, butter oil, which might well be a stand-in for the blood originally shed by a sacrificial animal.[4] To take another example from the Western tradition, the book of Leviticus in the Hebrew Bible – virtually a guidebook for priestly conduct – features especially the proper conduct of sacrificial acts; the festival events of ancient Judaism, and the very architecture of its temple, were organized around animal sacrifice.

Sacrifice is also a central theme in Judaism's most famous off-shoot, Christianity. The New Testament contains a sacrificial paradox, however, for its most holy figure largely eschews the role of priest; instead he plays the role of the sacrificed lamb.[5] The paragon of pathos that Jesus provides is a beacon to the whole of Christendom. According to Girard it is this identification with the sacrificial victim that makes Christianity unique.[6] It is also what makes sacrifice no longer necessary in Christianity, since Jesus, the perfect offering (and in Girard's terms, the perfect rival to oneself), has himself ended the spiral of competition between oneself and one's ideal rival that leads to the violence that requires new sacrificial scapegoats.

Perhaps for that reason – or simply because of the trivialization that comes with familiarity – in modern-day Christianity the sacrifice of Jesus is sentimentalized. One wonders that familiarity can prevent Christians from being repulsed by the central symbol of the faith: an execution device from which, at least in the Catholic tradition, the dying body still hangs. In some versions of the symbol, such as in Latin American Catholicism, the images are bloody indeed. And yet they are safely bloody. They are such caricatures of crucifixion that they domesticate the act; so too do such pious and comforting Protestant hymns as 'The Old Rugged Cross', 'Washed in the Blood of the Lamb', and 'There is a Fountain Flowing with Blood'. In conjuring up the terrible event of Christ's execution, the image is artistically diffused: the awful image is softened and the memory of it is eased by theological interpretations.

The idea of a hero, like Jesus, offering him or herself as a sacrificial victim is not unique to Christianity. Self-sacrifice – martyrdom – may be found in several ancient traditions. An early version of this idea is to be found in the Jewish notion of kiddush hashem (purification through holding true to the name of God). When faced with an oppressor, Jewish leaders would defend the faith to their deaths rather than betray their allegiance to it, and by so doing they became sanctified. The whole of the nation Israel became sanctified in the suffering role – implicitly the sacrificial victim's role – foreseen by prophets such as Isaiah. This theme in the Hebrew Bible no doubt had a great deal of influence on the New Testament's notion of self-sacrifice, and it was probably also in the background of the early Christian Church's concept of sainthood. The word 'saint' means having become sacred; and the first Christians to be sanctified in that way were the Christian martyrs persecuted by the Romans.

With these Jewish and Christian themes to precede it, it is no surprise that in Muslim thought martyrdom also became a prominent motif. Nowhere is this more pronounced than in Shiite Islam, where the memorial day of the suffering of the martyr Husain is the central festival of the tradition. During the month of Muharram, Shiites throughout the world parade through city streets, flagellating themselves with whips and, in some cases, with barbed wire, reminding themselves of the suffering of their victim hero.

Sikhism, an offshoot of medieval devotional Hinduism that flourished in a region of northern India dominated by Muslim rule, may well have been influenced by the Islamic notion of martyrdom. The concept is central to the faith. One of the ten gurus who founded the tradition – Guru Tegh Bahadur – is perceived as a martyr to hostile Mogul forces, and many of the most glorified heroes in Sikh history were martyred as well. One of these was Baba Deep Singh, whom modern religious artists portray as being so valiant in his struggle against the foes of Sikhism that he fought on even after his head was severed from his body. With such a reputation, it should not be surprising that the most recent leader of the order founded by him became a martyr as well. Baba Deep Singh's spiritual descendent, Jernail Singh Bhindranwale, led a militant band of Sikhs in a seemingly suicidal mission against Prime Minister Indira Gandhi; he was himself killed in her army's invasion of Sikhism's major shrine, the Golden Temple at Amritsar. In retaliation, Mrs Gandhi was assassinated – some pious Indians would say martyred – a few months later.

Soon after Mrs Gandhi's death, villagers from the rural areas surrounding Delhi came in long lines to her house to give offerings in front of pictures of the fallen leader as they would to images of a temple goddess. The reason why some Hindus could regard Mrs Gandhi as a marytr is that Hinduism has a precedent for such a concept. In the act of *sati*, when a widow throws herself on the funeral pyre of her dead husband, she becomes sanctified. Indeed, she becomes virtually a god.[7]

There are differences, however, between the martyrdom of the Hindu widow on the funeral pyre and the martyrdom of Baba Deep Singh. The most obvious one is that the latter takes place in a time of war. Is it appropriate to speak of martyrdom on the battlefield as a sacrificial act? If so, the lines have blurred between symbolic and real violence, and between sacredotal and political events.

It seems to me that the line between the symbolic and the real is frequently a blurry affair, and that the themes of sacrifice, martyrdom and religious warfare intertwine in virtually every religious tradition. They are conceptually linked. They are all about destruction, of course, but more importantly they are about human destruction on behalf of a divine purpose. For that reason, they are related; each can be explained in terms of the others. Sacrifice can be regarded as a symbolic form of warfare or as symbolic form of noble self-destruction (martyrdom); martyrdom can be seen as the internalization of sacrifice or of war; and religious warfare can be viewed as a litany of sacrifice and martyrdom. But which is primary and which are secondary?

From Girard's point of view, it is sacrifice that is basic, for it symbolically portrays a horrible and hidden desire. This is the longing to

conquer and destroy something (or rather, someone) intimately similar
to oneself: one's rival. The rival is one who, in Girard's terms, 'serves
as a model for the subject [oneself], not only in regard to such secondary
matters as style and opinions but also, and more essentially, in regard
to desires'.[8] To conquer the rival one has to destroy it. But before one
does, the rival will fight back, and thus will begin a hideous spiral of
reprisals and counterviolence. To prevent this, and the rift in the social
fabric that occurs when one's rivals are one's own friends and kinfolk,
one seeks a sacrificial victim who can symbolically stand in for the rival
and deflect the brunt of the violence.

Thus, in Girard's view, sacrifice is basic to human interaction because
it is an expression of an even more basic human need: identity. One
wants to understand one's self, and in order to do so one identifies
with an idealized other, who becomes one's rival. The identification
with one's rival and the craving for whatever the rival craves is what
Girard calls 'mimetic desire', the desire to imitate. He regards it as a
fundamental aspect of the human condition; mimetic desire in Girard's
reckoning is virtually instinctual.

This explanation for the origins of sacrifice is hauntingly familiar.
Freud advances a similar thesis in *Totem and Taboo*, although here the
motor that drives the sacrificial vehicle is not mimetic desire but oedipal
aggression.[9] Freud thought that human nature possessed a destructive
instinct, and to keep it from tearing apart a family or tribe or civil society,
its violence had to be visited upon a sacrificial foe. Freud concluded that
this violent streak was not just destructive but self-destructive, a form
of thanatos, a death wish. This desire to purify oneself through suicide
was for him a sort of martyrdom, and in that sense one could say that
Freud regarded martyrdom as the primary impulse. Violence aimed at
another person and the sacrificial acts that are devised to contain it are
the consequences.

One might ask whether Freud was right in thinking that aggression and
self-destruction are instinctual building-blocks of the human condition,
and Girard raises this and other questions in his penetrating analysis
of Freud in *Violence and the Sacred*.[10] One could also question, in
turn, whether Girard was right in the concepts he chose to replace
Freud's. I do not see that Girard's mimetic desire is more basic to the
human condition, or more all-encompassing as a motive for violence,
than Freud's instincts of aggression and sexual competition.

For the moment, however, let us say that the matter cannot be easily
settled, and that Freud and Girard may be equally right in their
attributions of a motive for violent behavior. Moving away from the
subject of motivation, and returning to the displacement of violence

and the role that religion plays in it, according to both Freud and Girard, symbolic sacrifice is the primary mechanism for displacing violence.

In considering an alternative to theories of symbolic displacement based on sacrifice, my hypothesis is that images of religious warfare are prior to both sacrifice and martyrdom in the mechanism of symbolically displacing violence, and that the motivation behind the creation of these images of spiritual war is a basic longing for order.

Religious Language and the Language of Ultimate Order

Soon after the outbreak of the Gulf War on 16 January 1991, religious television programs throughout the United States capitalized on the theme and drew parallels between the conflict and the spiritual struggle of everyday life. One television evangelist dressed up in desert battle fatigues and stood in front of a battle bivouac set. 'There is a war going on', he sternly warned his viewers, explaining that 'the devil has invaded our minds and hearts with bad thoughts and fear of the unknown.'[11] Only a fully-fledged spiritual assault comparable to that of the allied forces in Operation 'Desert Storm', he implied, would be able to liberate the soul.

This television evangelist is hardly an anomaly among preachers of most religious faiths. The rhetoric of warfare is as prominent in modern religious vocabulary as is the language of sacrifice, and virtually all cultural traditions are filled with martial metaphors. The ideas of a Salvation Army in Christianity and a Dal Khalsa ('Army of the faithful') in Sikhism, for instance, are used to characterize a disciplined religious organization. Images of spiritual warfare are even more common. The Muslim notion of jihad is the most noticable example, but Protestant preachers everywhere encourage their flocks to wage war against the forces of evil. Their homilies might be followed with hymns that speak of becoming like 'Christian soldiers', fighting 'the good fight', and struggling 'manfully onward'.

In a recent Ph.D. dissertation submitted to Harvard University, the author, Harriet Crabtree, surveyed the images that are prominent in what she called the 'popular theologies' projected in the hymns, tracts and sermons of modern Protestant Christianity. She finds the 'model of warfare' to be prominent.[12] What is significant, Crabtree states, is that the image is meant to be taken in a more than metaphorical way. Not only do the writers of hymns urge 'soldiers of the Cross' to 'stand up, stand up for Jesus' symbolically, but in a real, albeit spiritual, combat. Preachers and religious writers such as Arthur Wallis claim that 'Christian living *is* war'. Wallis explains that the warfare is not 'a metaphor or a figure of speech' but a 'literal fact'; the character of the war, however – 'the sphere, the weapons, and the foe – are spiritual rather than material'.[13]

In earlier times warfare was at least as common to religion as sacrificial rites; perhaps more so. Whole books of the Hebrew Bible are devoted to the military exploits of great kings, their contests relayed in gory detail. The New Testament does not take up the battle cry immediately, but the later history of the Church does, supplying a Christian record of bloody crusades and religious wars. In India, warfare is part of the grandeur of mythology. The great epics, the Ramayana and the Mahabharata, are seemingly unending tales of conflict and military intrigue. These epics, more than Vedic rituals, define subsequent Hindu culture. The indigenous name for India, Bharata, comes from the epics, as does the name, Sri Lanka, given to Ceylon by its people after independence. The epics continue to live in contemporary southern Asia. The soap opera versions of the epics produced in the mid-1980s were the most popular television series ever aired in India (and, considering that country's vast population, perhaps the most-watched television series in history).

Even cultures that do not have a strong emphasis on sacrifice have persistent images of religious war. In Sri Lanka, for example, Sinhalese legendary history as recorded in the Pali Chronicles, the *Dipavamsa* and the *Mahavamsa* – which have assumed almost canonical status in Sri Lankan society – amounts to a triumphal record of great battles waged by legendary Buddhist kings.

The interesting thing about the battles of the *Mahavamsa*, the Bible and the Hindu epics is that they are generally not moral struggles; unlike the Manichaean notion of a cosmic conflict between good and evil, these battles testify to a different sort of ultimate encounter. The motif that runs through these mythic and legendary scenes of warfare is the theme of 'us' versus 'them': the known versus the unknown. In the battles of the Bible and such epics as the Ramayana, the enemy are often foreigners who come from the shady edges of known civilization: places like Babylonia or Lanka. These murky foes embody some of the conceptual ambivalence of their locations: that is, they stand in for what is chaotic and uncertain about the world, including those things that defy categorization altogether. In cases where the enemy possesses a familiar face – as in the Mahabharata, where the war is between sets of cousins – the theme of chaos is carried out by the battle itself. It is the wickedness of warfare that the battle depicts, as the mythic figure Arjuna observes at the outset of his encounter with Lord Krishna on the battlefield.[14] To fight in such a circumstance is to assent to the disorder of this world, knowing that in a grander sense this disorder is corrected by a cosmic

order that is beyond killing and being killed. Such is the message of
Lord Krishna in his colloquy to Arjuna that is called the *Bhagavad
Gita*.[15] Ultimately such struggles are battles against the most chaotic
aspect of reality: death.[16]

Crabtree asserts that the image of warfare is attractive because it
'situates the listener or reader in the religious cosmos'.[17] This is true,
but the opposite is also the case: the sense of being situated in a religious
cosmos leads naturally to images of warfare. The reason this is so is that
religious rhetoric always, ultimately, affirms the primacy of order. In
order to affirm the primacy of order, it must conquer disorder, and
nothing is more disorderly than violence. Thus religious harmony and
violent disruption are locked together in a cosmic struggle. Religion
must deal with violence, not only because violence is unruly and
has to be tamed, but because religion, as the ultimate statement of
meaningfulness, has always to assert the primacy of meaning in the
face of chaos. For that reason, also, religion is order-restoring and
life-affirming even though it may justify the taking of life in particular
instances, as when a heroic or sacrificial act is seen as tipping the balance
of power and allowing a struggle for order to succeed.

This notion of religion as the grand purveyor of order in the world
is not my view alone. The recent attempts of a number of scholars to
find a definition of religion that is not specific to any cultural region
or historical period have also settled on meaningfulness and order as
religion's defining characteristic. As my earlier article on this topic
observed, these definitions reach for ways of stating that religion gives
significance to the inchoate and unruly aspects of daily life.[18] Clifford
Geertz, for instance, sees religion as the effort to integrate everyday
reality into a pattern of coherence that takes shape on a deeper level.[19]
Robert Bellah also thinks of religion as the attempt to reach beyond
ordinary reality in the 'risk of faith' that allows people to act 'in the
face of uncertainty and unpredictability'.[20] Peter Berger specifies that
such faith is an affirmation of the sacred, which acts as a doorway to a
different kind of reality.[21] Louis Dupre prefers to avoid the term 'sacred',
but integrates elements of both Berger's and Bellah's definitions into his
description of religion as 'a commitment to the transcendent as to *another
reality*'.[22]

What all of these definitions have in common is their emphasis
on a certain experience of meaningfulness shared within particular
communities over a long period of time. It is an experience of a
stratum of reality deeper than the one we know in everyday life. As
Durkheim, whose thought is fundamental to each of these thinkers,
was adamant in observing, religion has a more encompassing force

than can be suggested by any dichotomization of the sacred and the profane. To Durkheim, the religious point of view includes both the notion that there is such a dichotomy, and that the sacred aspects of it will always, ultimately, dominate the profane.[23] Following Durkheim, and incorporating elements from the above definitions of religion, religion could be described as the shared perception that there is a difference between reality as it appears and as it really is (or has been, or will be), and the shared conviction that the real order does (or will) ultimately reign supreme.

This definition helps us think of religion as a kind of language, or a way of looking at the world, rather than as an experience or a set of beliefs.[24] When we talk of the various 'religions', then, we mean the communities that have a tradition of sharing a particular set of images and terms for speaking about meaningful things in the world. The use of religious language (or rather, the language of religion) implies that there is more to life than appearances suggest; or to put it another way, that there is an essential conflict between appearance and deeper reality. The religious way of thinking implies that the deeper reality holds a degree of permanence and order quite unobtainable by ordinary means. As many religious people would affirm, the city of God is more real than any made by humans. Yet as Durkheim reminds us, the sphere of religion is not just the sacred realm alone, it is both sacred and profane areas of existence; it is the sacred encompassing the profane. The conflict between the two is what religion is about: religious language contains images both of grave disorder and tranquil order, bound together in a cosmic struggle. It often holds out the hope that despite appearances to the contrary, order eventually will triumph, and disorder will be contained.

There is nothing in this view that requires religion to be violent, but it does lead one to expect religious language to make sense of violence and to incorporate it in some way into the world view it expresses. Violence, after all, shocks one's sense of order and has the potential for causing the ultimate disorder in any person's life: physical destruction and death. Since religious language is about the tension between order and disorder, it is frequently about violence.

Religious images allow for peace and order to conquer violence and chaos; so it is understandable that the violence religion portrays is in some way limited or tamed – for instance, in the normalcy with which the Christians' eucharist is eaten and their blood-filled hymns are sung. In ritual, violence is symbolically transformed. The blood of the eucharistic wine is ingested by the supplicant and becomes part of living tissue; it brings new life. In song a similarly calming transformation occurs as the images are ingested aurally. For as Christian theology explains, in Christ violence has been bridled. Christ died in order for death to be defeated, and his blood is sacrificed so that his faithful followers will be rescued from a punishment as gruesome as his.

Other religious traditions deal with violence in much the same way. In the Sikh tradition, for instance, the two-edged sword provides an image of the domestication of violence. This familiar symbol is worn on lockets and proudly emblazoned on shops and garden gates. It is at the forefront of worship centers in Sikh *gurdwaras*, where it is treated as reverently as Christians treat their own emblem of destruction and triumph, the cross. Other images of violence in Sikhism also function like their counterparts in Christianity: the gory wounds of Sikh martyrs, like those of Christian saints, bleed on in calendar art, reminding the faithful that because their blood was shed, the faithful need fear no harm. Sikh theologians and writers, like their Christian counterparts, are eager to explain the meaning of such symbols and stories allegorically. They point toward the war between belief and unbelief that rages in each person's soul. In a similar way, interpreters of Jewish and Islamic culture have transformed the martial images in their traditions. The chroniclers of the Hebrew Bible saw acts of war as God's vengeance. So too have Muslim historians; and some Islamic mystics speak of the true jihad as the one within each person's soul.

Rituals of sacrifice fit into this general pattern of religious rhetoric: they are enactments of cosmic war. Like the enemy in a religious battle, the sacrifical victim is often ambiguous or categorically out of place, and is therefore a symbol of disorder. Animals used for sacrifice, for instance, are usually domestic beasts, and are for that reason in the ambiguous middle ground between the animal kingdom and the human. If the victim is human, he is frequently also from an ambiguous category: a captured enemy made into a member of the household, for instance – a phenomenon that occurred among Huron and Seneca Indians.[25] Or, as in the case of Amal martyrs in Lebanon, the sacrificial victims are unmarried men of marriageable age.[26] In the case of the *sati* conducted by Indian widows, the victims are inauspicious anomalies: married women bereft of living husbands. Sometimes it is God himself or herself who is offered up, or a divinely inspired person such as Jesus or Husain, whose very existence is an anomaly. It is not their sacrifice that makes them divine; their almost unhuman holiness is precisely what makes them candidates for sacrifice.[27]

Thus images of sacrifice, like other symbols of violence in religion, are ordinarily symbols of a violence conquered – or at least put in place – by the larger framework of order that religious language provides. But if religious images are supposed to conquer violence, one must ask the obvious but difficult question: why and how are these symbolic presentations of violence occasionally linked to real acts of violence? Ordinarily they should prevent violent acts by allowing the urges to conquer and control to be channelled into the harmless dramas of ritual. Yet we know that the opposite is sometimes the case. The violence of religion can be savagely real.

When the Cosmic War Becomes Real

What about real acts of religious violence? The death squads of Sikh and Sinhalese revolutionaries, the terrorist acts of Lebanese and Egyptian Muslims, and the religious soldiers of militant Jewish and Christian activists are all engaged in violence in direct and significantly non-symbolic ways. At first glance it would appear that their actions do not result in the peaceful displacement of disorder that ritualized forms of religious violence produce. At second glance, however, it would appear that some of these real cases of violence fit the pattern after all, when the violence is committed in a ritualized and symbolic way. Some of the acts themselves – such as the hijacking of American planes by Muslim terrorists and the murder of a busload of Hindu pilgrims in the Himalayan foothills by a band of radical Sikh youths – are done dramatically. These are abnormal, illegal, shocking acts that are done with the intention of vividly displaying the destructive power of violence.

All acts of killing are violent, of course, but unlike murder committed in the context of ordinary warfare or capital punishment, these acts seem deliberately designed to elicit feelings of revulsion and anger from those who witness them.[28] In some cases the killing has taken the form of religious sacrifice.[29] Yet most of these acts of religious violence are less like sacrifice than they are like war. Of course one can think of religious warfare as a blend of sacrifice and martyrdom, or even as an exchange between the two, where one sacrifices members of the enemy's side and offers up martyrs on one's own. But behind this gruesome litany is something that encompasses both sacrifice and martyrdom: the triumph of sacred order over the disorder of the profane world.

There is a difference between wars justified by religion, however, and religious wars. It is one thing when the moral sanction of religion is brought to bear on such worldly and non-spiritual matters as political struggles. It is quite another when the struggles themselves are seen primarily as religious events. The crusades, for instance, are examples from Christian history when a military expedition was carried out with religious zeal. To engage in such a struggle was a salvific act. Many of the present-day religious revolutions are conducted with the same spiritual intensity, and are regarded as carrying a similar power of salvation for those who take part in them. These revolutionary activities are not just political exercises justified by religion, they are perceived by the faithful as facets of a more fundamental confrontation. Conflicts in the real world are linked to an invisible, cosmic war: the spiritual struggle between order and disorder, light and darkness, faith and doubt.

When the militant Sikh leader, Jernail Singh Bhindranwale, exhorted his followers to action, his rhetoric was crowned with the image of struggle: a 'struggle . . . for our faith, for the Sikh nation, for the oppressed . . .'.[30] On the personal level it was the tension between faith and the lack of faith; on the cosmic level it was the battle between truth and evil. Often his rhetoric was vague about who the enemy really was. 'In order to destroy religion', Bhindranwale informed his congregation, 'mean tactics have been initiated', and they came from 'all sides and in many forms'.[31] But rather than explain what these forces were, who were behind them, and why they would want to destroy religion, Bhindranwale dwelled instead on what should be the response: a willingness to fight and defend the faith – if necessary, to the end. 'Young men: with folded hands, I beseech you', Bhindranwale implored, reminding them that the ultimate decision between truth and evil was up to them.[32] Since the cosmic war is waged against disorder, it is understandable that the foes are amorphous; they are, in fact, symbols for amorphousness itself.

This link between a worldly struggle and the cosmic one is found in the rhetoric of other religious activists as well. 'Life is faith and struggle', says Khomeini, indicating that the notion of fighting is basic to human existence, and on a par with religious commitment.[33] Khomeini's one-time associate, Banisadr, wrote at some length about the notion of struggle in Islam, explaining how, although the monotheism of Islam will not allow for the notion of a struggle between the world and the spirit – for it does not recognize that duality – it does allow for a struggle against duality itself.[34] When Khomeini and Banisadr talk about the struggle against evil and injustice in these vague terms, they are at home with preachers in every religious tradition who speak about the need to struggle against a generalized sense of falsehood and unbelief.

What makes the language of Banisadr and Khomeini different from the language used by many of their fellow preachers in Islam and elsewhere is that they see the struggle occurring on a social and political plane. When Khomeini prays to his 'noble God for protection from the evil of every wicked traitor' and asks Him to 'destroy the enemies', he has particular traitors and enemies in mind.[35] His list of the 'satanic' forces that are out to destroy Islam include Jews, of course, but also the even 'more satanic' Westerners. When he refers to these evil Westerners Khomeini is not speaking of Christians, particularly, but of merchants, politicians and corporate leaders with 'no religious belief' who see Islam as 'the major obstacle in the path of their materialistic ambitions and the chief threat to their political power'.[36] Prior to the Iranian revolution, the Shah was understood as a companion of these satanic forces and a tool of colonialists.[37] As in the case of the radical Sikhs' enemies, the Ayatollah's foes are often vaguely described.

Interestingly the Ayatollah's diatribes identify American colonialism as a threat to Islamic faith as well as to social and political interests: 'All the problems of Iran and of the Moslems are the work of the foreign colonialists and the work of America', Khomeini asserts.[38] On another occasion, the Ayatolloh blends political, personal and spiritual issues together in generalizing about the cosmic foes – now described as Western colonialism – and about 'the black and dreadful future' which 'the agents of colonialism, may God Almighty abandon them all', have in mind for Islam and the Muslim people.[39]

Christians supporting the Sandinista revolutionary struggle in Nicaragua also perceived their opponents as being more than political enemies: they were cosmic foes, sometimes amorphously described. Their's were not just ordinary political conflicts, they implied, but conflicts that had sacral dimensions. Ernesto Cardenal explains that the revolutionary struggle in Nicaragua was 'totally different from the case of political parties that are all trying to come to power' in what he describes as 'a normalized, organized country', Cardenal searches for biblical metaphors in explaining what made the revolution in Nicaragua different: 'We're taking sides, yes – with the good Samaritan'. He goes on to say that 'here you have to take sides, you have to be partisan. Either you're with the slaughtered or you're with the slaughterers. From a gospel point of view I don't think there was any other legitimate option we could have made'.[40]

In Sri Lanka, the metaphors of sacred struggle are drawn from Buddhist theology. 'We live in a time of *dukkha*', a militant bhikkhu explained.[41] As he elaborated this point it became clear that he was more than simply restating the first of the Four Noble Truths, that all life is suffering. In the bhikkhu's mind the concept of suffering – *dukkha* – had a definite social significance. 'We live in an immoral world', he stated, using the term *adhammic*, which can also be translated as 'disorderly' or 'irreligious'. Behind the notion is the conflict between *dhamma* and *adhamma* – order and disorder, religion and irreligion – and by invoking that image, he couched the political concerns that he and other Buddhist activists in Sri Lanka have expressed in the most ultimate of terms.

Right-wing Jewish activists in Israel also use the images of cosmic war to justify their actions. Rabbi Meir Kahane, for instance, speaks of God's vengeance against the Gentiles which began with the humiliation of the Pharaoh in the Exodus from Egypt over three thousand years ago and continues today with the humiliation of the Gentiles that results in the creation of Israel.[42] 'When the Jews are at war', Kahane says, 'God's name is great'.[43] An Israeli activist who was once arrested for his participation in a plot to blow up the Muslim's Dome of the Rock in Jerusalem echoes Kahane's words, and claims that 'God always fights against His enemies', adding that activists such as himself 'are the instruments of this fight'.[44] Once again, the identity of the enemy – like the cosmic foe itself – is beyond any easy description or demarcation.

Summary

In the rhetoric of religious activists in Israel, Iran, India, Nicaragua, Sri Lanka and elsewhere, it is the image of warfare, rather than sacrifice, that is most frequently invoked in describing and justifying contemporary instances of religious violence. Elsewhere I develop at length the implications of this invocation and attempt to show why religious language is easily exploited for political purposes by activists seeking a moral justification for violence, and why religion is part of new nationalist movements world wide.[45] Many of these movements are violent in their rejection of secular nationalism in favor of more culturally specific forms of democracy. Cosmic warfare, in these cases, is more than just a metaphor; it is the grand context in which all of life's struggles, including political ones, make sense. Cosmic war and real war become one.

This article has tried to show that violent images are endemic to religious ways of thinking because of the nature of religion. At the heart of religious language is the attempt to impose order on disorder. The effort to impose order involves the encompassing of chaos by a grander scheme, and this means that images of chaos (including the most chaotic things imaginable, violence and death) must be conjured up so that chaos may be contained. It also means that there is sometimes the perception of an encounter between the two, order and disorder; it is a struggle that is frequently imagined as proceeding on a cosmic plane. It is when this cosmic war is confused with a struggle in the social world that religious violence becomes savagely real.

This is a somewhat different explanation of religious violence than the one offered by Girard. But my point of view does affirm the value of many of Girard's insights, including his suggestion that violence may be displaced symbolically through sacrificial rites. When these rituals help to defuse violent impulses – including especially those associated with notions of religious war – they are indeed blessed acts.

NOTES

1. René Girard, *Violence and the Sacred*, trans. by Patrick Gregory (Baltimore, MD and London: The Johns Hopkins University Press, 1977), orig. published as *La violence et le sacre* (Paris: Éditions Bernard Grasset, 1972).
2. Ibid., p.40.
3. See my 'The Logic of Religious Violence,' in David Rapoport (ed.), *Inside Terrorist Organizations*, (London: Frank Cass, and New York, NY: Columbia University Press, 1988), pp.172–192; and my 'What the Bhikkhu Said: Reflections on the Rise of Militant Religious Nationalism,' *Religion*, Vol. 20, (Spring 1990), pp.53–75.
4. See J. Frits Staal, in collaboration with C. V. Somayajipad and M. Itti Ravi Nambudiri, *Agni: The Vedic Ritual of the Fire Altar*, Vol. 1, (Berkeley, CA: Asian Humanities Press, 1983), p.18.
5. While the theme of Christ as suffering servant is dominant in the Christian tradition, its theology is not entirely united on this point. The book of Hebrews in the New Testament, for instance, portrays Jesus as both priest and sacrifical offering.
6. See René Girard, *The Scapegoat* (Baltimore, MD and London: The Johns Hopkins Press, 1986) (orig. pub. as *Le bouc emissaire*, Paris: Grasset, 1985).
7. For explanations for the continuing significance of *sati* in India today, see John Stratton Hawley (ed.), *New Light on Sati* (New York, NY: Oxford University Press, forthcoming).
8. Girard, *Violence and the Sacred*, p.145.
9. For Girard's perceptive and appreciative critique of Freud in general and *Totem and Taboo* in particular, see *Violence and the Sacred*, pp.169–222.
10. Ibid.
11. Rev. Wayne E. Anderson, 'Battle Cry' television program, KWHE-TV, Channel 14, Honolulu, I, 30 Jan. 1991.
12. Harriet Crabtree, 'The Quest for True Models of the Christian Life: An Evaluative Study of the Use of Traditional Metaphor in Contemporary Popular Theologies of the Christian Life,' Ph.D. dissertation, Harvard University, 1989. Her findings with regard to warfare are summarized in her article, 'Onward Christian Soldiers? The Fortunes of a Traditional Christian Symbol in the Modern Age,' *Bulletin of the Center for the Study of World Religion, Harvard University*, Vol. 16, No 2, (1989–90), pp.6–27.
13. Quoted in Crabtree, 'Onward Christian Soldiers', p.10. The italics are in the original.
14. *Bhagavad Gita*, Ch. 1, verse 45.
15. *Bhagavad Gita*, Ch. 2, verses 19–34.
16. Ibid. As Ernst Becker has observed in *The Denial of Death* and *Escape from Evil*, religious imagination serves to enlarge one's sense of the potential for life and deny death altogether. Although in general I agree with Becker, he is not right in every case: it is possible to employ the language of sacrifice, marytrdom and warfare to reassert the primacy of structure over chaos in general, rather than death in particular.
17. Crabtree, 'Onward Christian Soldiers', p.7.
18. Juergensmeyer, 'The Logic of Religious Violence,' p.178.
19. Clifford Geertz defines religion as 'a system of symbols which acts to establish powerful, pervasive and long-lasting moods and motivations in men by formulating conceptions of a general order of existence and clothing these conceptions with

such an aura of factuality that the moods and motivations seem uniquely realistic' ('Religion as a Cultural System', reprinted in William A. Lessa and Evon Z. Vogt, eds., *Reader in Comparative Religion: An Anthropological Approach*, 3rd ed. (New York, NY: Harper and Row, (1972), p.168.
20. Robert Bellah, 'Transcendence in Contemporary Piety,' in Donald R. Cutler, *The Religious Situation: 1969*, (Boston, MA: Beacon Press, 1969), p.907.
21. Peter Berger, *The Heretical Imperative* (New York: Doubleday, 1980), p.38. See also his *Sacred Canopy: Elements of a Sociological Theory of Religion* (Garden City, NY: Doubleday, 1967).
22. Louis Dupre, *Transcendent Selfhood: The Loss and Rediscovery of the Inner Life*, (New York, NY: Seabury Press, 1976, p.26. For a discussion of Berger and Dupre's definitions, see Mary Douglas, 'The Effects of Modernization on Religious Change', *Daedalus*, Vol. 111, No. 1 (Winter 1982), pp.1–19.
23. Durkheim describes the dichotomy of sacred and profane in religion in the following way: 'In all the history of human thought there exists no other example of two categories of things so profoundly differentiated or so radically opposed to one another. . . . The sacred and the profane have always and everywhere been conceived by the human mind as two distinct classes, as two worlds between which there is nothing in common . . . In different religions, this opposition has been conceived in different ways' (Emile Durkheim, *The Elementary Forms of the Religious Life*, trans by Joseph Ward Swain (London: Allen & Unwin., 1976), [orig. published in 1915], pp.38–39). Durkheim goes on to talk about the sacred things that religions encompass; but the first thing he says about the religious view is the perception that there is this dichotomy.
24. On this point I am in agreement with Wilfred Cantwell Smith who suggested some years ago that the noun 'religion' might well be banished from our vocabulary, and that we restrict ourselves to using the adjective 'religious': *The Meaning and End of Religion: A New Approach to the Religious Traditions of Mankind* (New York, NY: The Macmillan Company, 1962), pp.119–53. In the terminology suggested by George Lindbeck in *The Nature of Doctrine*, my understanding of religion is 'cultural-linguistic' rather than 'experiential-expressive'.
25. Anthony F. C. Wallace, *The Death and Rebirth of the Seneca* (New York, NY: Random House, 1969), pp.102–7.
26. See Martin Kramer's article in this volume.
27. Herman Melville's *Billy Budd* trades on this same theme. In a recent book of essays on sainthood and morality, the authors consistently come to a similar conclusion, that social misfits make good candidates for sainthood. They must be perceived as 'sublimely wacky' in order for their martyrdom and self-sacrifice to be seen as saintly. See John Stratton Hawley (ed.), *Saints and Virtues* (Berkeley, CA: University of California Press, 1987).
28. For an interesting discussion of the definition of violence and terror in political contexts see Thomas Perry Thornton, 'Terrorism as a Weapon of Political Agitation', in Harry Eckstein (ed.), *Internal War: Problems and Approaches* (New York, NY: The Free Press, 1964), and David C. Rapoport, 'The Politics of Atrocity', in Y. Alexander and S. Finger (eds), *Terrorism: Interdisciplinary Perspectives* (New York, NY: John Jay, 1977).
29. See the article by Martin Kramer in this volume.
30. Jernail Singh Bhindranwale, 'Two Lectures Given on 19 July and 20 Sept. 1983', transcribed and translated into English from the videotaped originals in Punjab by Ranbir Singh Sandhu and distributed by the Sikh Religious and Educational Trust, Columbus, OH, 1986, p.2.
31. Jernail Singh Bhindranwale, 'Address to the Sikh Congregation', a sermon given in the Golden Temple in Nov. 1983, transcribed and translated from the audiotape original in Punjab by Ranbir Singh Sandhu, distributed by the Sikh Religious and Educational Trust, Columbus, OH, 1985, p.1.
32. Bhindranwale, 'Two Lectures', p.22.

33. Ayatollah Khomeini, *Collection of Speeches, Position Statements*, translations from 'Najaf Min watha 'iq al-Imam al-Khomeyni did al-Quwa al Imbiriyaliyah wa al-Sahyuniyah wa al-Raj'iyah' From the Papers of Imam Khomeyni Against Imperialist, Zionist and Reactionist Powers), 1977; translations on Near East and North Africa, Number 1902 (Arlington, Va: Joint Publications Research Service, 1979), p.6.
34. Banisadr, pp.28–35.
35. Khomeini, *Collection*, p.30.
36. Imam [Ayatollah] Khomeini, *Islam and Revolution: Writings and Declarations*, translated and annotated by Hamid Algar, (London: Routledge and Kegan Paul, 1985) [orig. published by Mizan Press, Berkeley, CA, 1981], pp.27–28.
37. *Collection*, p.24.
38. Ibid., p.3.
39. Ibid., p.25.
40. Ernesto Cardenal, in Teofilo Cabestrero, *Ministers of God, Ministers of the People: Testimonies of Faith from Nicaragua*, trans. from the Spanish by Robert R. Barr (Maryknoll, NY: Orbis Books, 1983), pp.22–23.
41. My interviews with the bhikkhu were conducted in Sri Lanka on 4–5 Feb. 1988, in English. For a fuller account, see my article, 'What the Bhikkhu Said'.
42. Rabbi Meir Kahane, speech on the announcement of the creation of the independent State of Judaea, Jerusalem, 18 Jan. 1989 (from my notes taken on that occasion).
43. Ibid.
44. Interview with Yoel Lerner, Jerusalem, 20 Jan. 1989.
45. See my articles, 'The Logic of Religious Violence' and 'What the Bhikkhu Said'. I am also developing this theme for a forthcoming book on the new religious nationalisms.

Some General Observations on Religion and Violence

DAVID C. RAPOPORT

Most people have been greatly astonished by the violence attending religious revivals of recent decades for it was commonly believed that religious revivals were associated with rekindling earnest passions for peace. The reasons were clear; the eschatologies of the revealed religions (Judaism, Christianity, and Islam) presume peace as the ultimate destiny of humanity, and a major theme or preoccupation of these religions is that one should seek peace whenever one can. Furthermore, particular sects (mostly within Christianity but not confined to it) interpret the teachings of their religion to mean that one should never use violence. In the great Indian religions, Hinduism, Buddhism, and Jainism, a reverence for all forms of life is fostered through the doctrine of *ahimsa*. The deeply religious Buddhist Emperor Asoka (third century BC) purportedly made non-violence a state policy, and among the Jainists some monks have carried the *ahimsa* ideal so far that they have starved themselves to death in order to avoid destroying life.

So striking was this disposition to peace that modern writers who discuss the sociological or political function of religion have almost always emphasized its 'violence-reducing' dimension. Thus, Marx describes religion as the 'opiate of the people', Freud contends that religion sublimates aggression, and Durkheim sees religion as an essential basis for community life.

Certainly, religion does have an *essential* violence-reducing element, but it also has a violence-producing dimension, one that is *equally* essential. The dichotomy is embodied in other related though not identical phenomena, those 'contradictory' traditions of 'quietism' and 'activism' and of subordination and resistance to authority which characterize

The earliest version of this paper was written for a Harry Frank Guggenheim Foundation Conference on Religion and Violence, Tuxedo Park, NY 1989. I am most grateful for the help of the Foundation in enabling me to complete it. Kees Bolle, Leonard Billet, Blair Campbell, Richard Hecht, Clark McCauley, and Maxwell Taylor read an earlier version and made helpful suggestions. My wife Barbara deserves special thanks; she read all the drafts and urged me to scrap earlier ones. The paper was presented at the XIIth World Congress of Sociology, Madrid, 9–13 July 1990.

most religions, especially the monotheistic ones. This double nature is seen vividly in all religious revivals where both 'peace movements' and bellicose activity are both stimulated. Because the focus here on the violence-producing character of religion may obscure the connections with peace, it might be useful to emphasize that in the final analysis, which will be the subject of another article, one element cannot be fully understood without relating it to the other.

In the process of discussing violence I shall enumerate various ways in which religion and violence may be related and note, *en passant*, the striking resemblances between religious and political communities on this issue. Examples will be drawn largely from the revealed religions, Judaism, Christianity, and Islam.

There are many reasons to believe that links between violence and religion exist, reasons which pertain to the character of the contemporary world, the nature of religion and that of violence. I will focus on areas relating to religion where we see such links. The areas are distinct, but connected and overlapping; and they represent different levels or kinds of analysis. The first three pertain to observations concerning the capacity of religions to inspire ultimate commitment, the language religions employ, and some contemporary speculations concerning the origin and nature of religions. I will move from the most obvious and least controversial to the least obvious and the most controversial. Then I want to deal with the issue of the religious revival and particularly with the apocalyptic or Messianic doctrines which are often associated with these revivals. Finally, I shall touch on a particular contemporary circumstance, namely, the desperation some believers feel that the spread of secular sentiments has gone so far that the time to deal with the predicament is running out. Little will be said about the nature of violence itself, though this is a matter of crucial importance.

The Capacity to Inspire Ultimate Commitment

Wars justified on religious grounds are common.[1] How, in view of the concerns of religion with peace, do we explain this? One pertinent point is that no major religion eschews violence under *all* conditions. In my own discipline, the history of political theory, while most traditional figures from the Greeks to the nineteenth century saw religion as indispensable for the education of good citizens and a harmonious political community, they also knew that good citizens will fight for their countries. Religion, then, could reduce violence and produce violence.

Machiavelli put this matter most forcefully. While all religions are not equal in this respect, experience and reason show that where religion exists there will inevitably be an enormous potentiality for 'good arms'. The Roman Republic had the most religious citizen body in the classical world, and that is why he thought they produced its most disciplined and effective soldiers.

Perhaps circumstances and context frame the disposition towards violence. But some relevant element seems to be inherent in the nature of religion itself. One such element is the capacity of religion to inspire total loyalties or commitments, and in this respect, it is difficult to imagine anything which surpasses the religious community. Religion has often had formidable rivals; in the modern world the nation sometimes has surpassed religion as a focus of loyalties, though significantly there is increasing propensity for academics to speak of 'civic religion' when discussing national symbols and rites. In any case, the ascendancy of the nation has occupied but a brief moment in history so far, and in a limited portion of the world – all of which only more underscores the durability and special significance of religion.

The belief that religion has a special capacity to generate emotions is incorporated into our vernacular. When, for example, we say of someone that 'baseball is his religion', we mean that he is committed to the game in an absolute fashion, that the game may obsess, perhaps even 'possess' him. At the very least, we are saying that he endows baseball with extraordinary importance. It may be significant, it is certainly not irrelevant, to remember that the word fan, (which seems so inseparable from the game of baseball) is a contraction of the word fanatic which itself comes from the Latin word for temple – *fanum*. The first definition of fanaticism in the *Oxford English Dictionary* refers to 'action or speech such as might result from the *possession* by a deity or demon', (my emphasis). When William James referred to religion as existing in the 'hot spot' of our brain, he was suggesting that it is the source of enormous energy, an energy expressed in enthusiasm and desperation, transforming otherwise mundane issues into matters of 'ultimate concern', to use Paul Tillich's often repeated pregnant phrase.

Words or concepts essential to the religious experience provide similar suggestions. A 'holy' man is one who is 'inviolable', 'morally or spiritually perfect', and 'free from sin'. To 'worship' is to 'adore', 'revere', and 'give (the deity) honors' deserved. A 'sacred' object is one put aside as especially dear to the deity', whose capacities in all respects are greater than our own.

> 'When I enter a church, a sacred space, I speak in whispers . . .
> By a kind of self-deprecation . . . I reduce my value somewhat and
> communicate sacrificed value to what is sacred . . . In exchange
> . . . I gain the charged blessing of what is sacred.[2]

I shall not try to explain why religion has this capacity. I shall simply accept its capacity to inspire ultimate commitment as a given, and comment on a few more conspicuous implications.

One such connotation is that the intensity of feeling which religions may arouse militates against the easy reconciliation of religious quarrels and invites violent solutions. Because religion can engender such intense feelings, a religious justification offered for a cause which might otherwise be justified in political or economic terms seriously influences the intensity of the violence used. Several years ago I demonstrated the point by comparing ancient sacred terror groups with modern secular ones, showing that the earlier ones, despite extraordinarily primitive technologies, were more destructive and durable.[3] Recent Rand Corporation statistics indicate that where religion has been the principal justification for contemporary terror, the results have been more deadly.[4] Wars of religion, it is commonly believed, are exceedingly ferocious and difficult to resolve,[5] and the foremost authority on genocide, Leo Kuper, has concluded that in virtually every case of genocide religious differences were an element.[6]

Because religion can command such loyalties, it will be manipulated by persons with secular causes. A striking example is a poem by Abraham (Yair) Stern, founder of Lehi, a secular Jewish terrorist group during the struggle for Israeli independence more familiar to the outside world as the 'Stern Gang'. The similes make the profane sacred, channeling the emotions and memories from venerated symbols and rituals unrelated to violence into activities which Stern deemed more productive.

> Like my father who carried his bag
> With a prayer shawl to the synagogue on the Sabbath
> So I will carry holy rifles in my bag
> To the prayer service of iron with a regenerated quorum
> Like my mother who lit candles on the festival eve
> So I will light a torch for those revered in praise
> Like my father who taught me to read in Torah
> I will teach my pupils; stand to arms, kneel and shoot
> Because there is a religion of redemption – a religion of the war
> of liberation
> Who ever accepts it – be blessed: whoever denies it – be cursed.[7]

This temptation to use religious language becomes even more enticing for a second reason. Religious communities are older and usually much more familiar to the general population than secular communities are; in fact, the latter often derive from the religious. Religion, therefore, may provide a good, and in some cases the only, way to communicate effectively with great portions of the population on intense emotional levels. Camus' play *Les Justes* offers an interesting example. Kaliev, the anarchist revolutionary, discovers that his socialist language is incomprehensible to the hangman Foka, who symbolizes the People. Kaliev then employs a religious parable; and even though the switch to another language occurs too late to be persuasive, Foka does begin to understand. Lawrence Durrell in *Bitter Lemons*, that remarkable memoir of the 1950s Cypriot uprising against the British, notes that as the campaign developed and enrolled greater and greater numbers, graffiti everywhere contained more and more religious imagery.

A most recent striking example of this process is provided by Saddam Hussein's effort to mobilize support against those attempting to make him leave Kuwait. He called for a jihad to 'expel the [Western] infidel' and 'to liberate from evil and occupation the sacred sites' in Saudi Arabia. A color photograph depicting a shirtless President Hussein kissing the shrine at Mecca and another of him in full military dress kneeling in prayer at that most sacred Islamic shrine alternated in the background as his speech was read'.[8] Since the crisis began in August 1990, his language has become saturated with religious references, which one veteran diplomat thought 'appeal(ed) to every Muslim at the basic level'.[9] The ironies here abound: a Christian founded Hussein's party (the Arab Ba'ath Socialist Party), the party made great strides in transforming Iraq into a secular state, and finally Hussein had just concluded a very costly war against Islamic fundamentalism.

It is relevant here, perhaps, to note that in many respects the religious differences which distinguish one group from its most dominant neighbor have created the bases for many ethnic communities and quite a few national ones too. This provides more evidence for the extraordinary salience of the religious bond.

Language and Life History

The second area where we see a link is the cultural manifestations of religion, or the actual content of the 'language' (using that term in the broadest possible sense) religious believers employ. Mark Juergensmeyer calls our attention to the point in 'The Logic of Religious Violence'.[10]

He reminds us that the major symbols, arts, rituals, sacred texts, and myths of all religions are full of violence; sometimes that violence is a violence suffered, othertimes it is a violence delivered, and in all cases the violence represents memories of desperate struggles in the past, and are literally 'trails of blood'. The violent character of those symbols suggests that a religion cannot survive, let alone grow, without developing extraordinary capacities to deal with the ultimate human predicaments of order and disorder and of good and evil. Normally, we can incorporate the memories of those early struggles in symbols which we can control. Religion, consequently, gives us means to domesticate dangerous passions or render them harmless. On the other hand, for reasons Juergensmeyer does not explain, sometimes the passions contained in the symbols are released and a renewal of the activity they have been restraining recurs.

If Juergensmeyer is correct, the histories of religions ought to illuminate this preoccupation, providing evidence of violent struggles in the earlier periods before texts, symbols, arts, rites, and myths were fully developed. He does not discuss the historical evidence, but a glance at Eliade's *Encyclopedia of Religion* (1987) and at Hasting's *Encyclopedia of Religion and Ethics* (1927) reveals that the articles devoted to war consume more than five times the space of those treating peace, that war was much more important in the older Indo-European religions (Graeco-Roman) than in the later ones (the revealed ones), and finally that war was especially critical in the formative period of particular religions.

Juergensmeyer's arguments strengthen the sense that the connection between religion and violence is essential not circumstantial; the very purpose of religion cannot be realized without developing the tools or mechanisms to restrain violence. But, one might ask, can one restrain violence without using coercion? If the answer is 'no', are we then denying that non-violence and violence are mutually exclusive conditions? It is a question I shall return to soon.

In any case, Juergensmeyer's observation provides a third reason (beyond importance and familiarity) for thinking that religion will attract violent men. Religious communities have developed 'special languages' to cope with violence or to make violence serve a public purpose. The vocabulary of the first secular rebel terrorists in Russia, for example, was saturated with Christian images and metaphors, especially those relating to the crucifixion, the resurrection and the Second Coming, all bloody and violent events. (Can one find more appropriate images for revolution than those showing how destruction can lead to rebirth?) The Russian terrorists understood that how one died was at least as critical for the success of one's cause as how one killed. Although most people believe that the passion of Christ which the Russians had in mind[11] demonstrates the futility of violence, symbols once developed can be used and interpreted in a variety of unexpected ways. Khachig Tololyan characterizes the history of Armenian terror since the nineteenth century as 'martyr-giving' and 'martyr-avenging', a description which is equally appropriate for the Russian case.[12]

Similar uses of language appear in other terrorist groups, though the particular images and metaphors vary from case to case and from religious tradition to religious tradition. Perinbaum's *Holy Violence*, shows, for example, how Fanon was influenced by the religious language of the secular Algerian FLN[13]. In the case of the Palestine Liberation Organization (which has always emphasized its secular character) the use of religious metaphors is striking, especially in *Fatah*, the PLO's largest and most important element:

> The imagery and symbol of *Fatah* is clear and strikingly Islamic. Yassir Arafat's *nom de guerre*, Abu'Ammar, the father of 'Ammar, is an allusion to the historic figure of 'Ammar ibn Yasir, the son of Yasir, a companion of the Prophet and a valiant fighter in all his battles. The name *Fatah* is a technical term, meaning a conquest for Islam. It is in this sense that Sultan Mehemet II, who conquered Constantinople for Islam is known as *Fatih*, the conqueror. The same image is carried over into the nomenclature of the Palestinian Liberation Army, the brigades of which are named after the great victories won by Muslim arms in the battles of *Qadisiyya*, *Hattin*, and *Ayn Jalut*. To name military units after victorious battles is by no means unusual. What is remarkable here is that all these battles were won in holy wars for Islam against non-Muslims – *Qadisiyya* against the Zoroastrian Persians, *Hattin* against the Crusaders, *Ayn Jalut* against the Mongols. In the second and third of these, the victorious armies were not even Arab; but they were Muslim and that is obviously what counts. It is hardly surprising that the military communiqués of the *Fatah* begins with the Muslim invocation, 'In the name of God, the Merciful and Compassionate'.[14]

One might also cite a rather interesting unexplained finding of Mostafa Reja's study of revolutionary leaders from 1640 to 1968: that the only universal feature in the makeup of revolutionaries was that each initially had formal religious affiliations. By itself this fact might seem trivial, but put in the context of the material we have been discussing, it reinforces the contention that religions create language to help one 'cope' with violence better.[15]

Origin and/or Purpose

So far, the two reasons offered for linking religion and violence have been based on appeals to common sense. The capacity of religion to inspire is familiar partly because the idea is embodied in the ways we use ordinary language. Once the discourse religion uses is called to our attention, some implications seem clear and easily verifiable.

Our third reason, or cluster of reasons, comes from crucial, though not easily demonstrated concerns, namely the origin and/or purpose of religion – a theme Juergensmeyer alludes to but never explicitly develops. Here one leans heavily on the authority of René Girard. His remarkable *Violence and the Sacred* is the only available systematic account of religion and violence, and one which is known, alas, much more among those in literary and textual studies than among social scientists.

Religion originates, Girard argues, in the attempt to cope with the failure of vengeance to stop the internal violence of kin-based societies. Furthermore, he stresses the fact, generally accepted by anthropologists, that the original rite of religion was itself a form of violence, namely – human sacrifice, an activity which Girard also labels 'collective murder'.[16] The genesis of religion indicates that its 'sole purpose is to prevent the recurrence of reciprocal violence'.[17] 'The function of ritual . . . is to keep violence *outside* the religious community'.[18]

Political theorists will find the general thrust of these arguments familiar, even if particular important details are not. Girard's conclusion resembles that of Hobbes and others in the discipline who argue that the immediate precipitating cause of the creation of the state is violence, and that the state in turn invents a special kind of violence, (to use Girard's language), namely the judiciary which is supposed to solve the problem which brought the state into being. Whether one accepts the details of Hobbes' formulation, virtually all social scientists agree that the state is distinguished by its unique relationship to violence, and this, it seems to me, is *the* crucial point.

Girard, of course, recognizes the kinship between religions and states, by suggesting that the state originates when a religion loses some of its effectiveness in curbing violence. In the final analysis, then, the judicial system and the institution of sacrifice share the same function, but the judicial system is infinitely more effective.[19]

The striking irony here, one formally unnoticed, is that although the state may originate in the effort to terminate violence, its capacity to discharge that function depends upon a profound social agreement concerning the source of legitimacy, an agreement which then makes it possible to employ violence on a scale hitherto unimaginable. The existence of peace, therefore, and the ability to make war are inseparable features of state life; and, in some respects, as we have suggested, one might characterize religion in a similar way.

Indeed, in some crucial respects, the capacity of religion to generate and control violence may be greater than that of the state. The state's adminstrative instruments are in principle more effective, but then in the long history of the state, religion has been an essential and quite possibly the most important ingredient in the state's legitimacy.

The attempt to ground the state wholly on secular principles (i.e the community rather than the deity authorizes law) is a relatively recent phenomenon dating only to the American and the French Revolutions. Could the current religious revivals reflect the fact that wholly secular principles of legitimacy are either inadequate or at most able to be sustained only in limited political contexts?

For Girard religion does not conquer violence with its opposite, that is by stimulating the peace-loving disposition or by demonstrating the horrors of violence. Violence is necessary to contain violence and hence, as suggested earlier, the non-violent and the violent states are not disconnected conditions. The logic animating religion and the state resembles that which inspires the vengeance of the kin society; the difference is in the results, because in the normal course of things the violence of religion and the state do not invite violence in response.[20] (Two moot questions, questions I cannot treat here, are, whether legitimate and illegitimate coercion should be described with the same term [i.e., violence], and, furthermore, whether one is entitled to think that a genetic account of the origins of an institution also establishes its purpose?) Nonetheless, Girard's explanation of the kinship between religion and the state helps us understand better why those indifferent or hostile to religion still find its language so attractive.

There are, however, some major differences between Girard and the tradition of political thought which Hobbes represents. For Girard religion was created to justify human sacrifice precisely because humans could not accept responsibility for the fact that they could not sustain community without sacrifices. The legitimacy of primitive religion depends upon maintaining a stupendous collective self-deception. 'Violence is the heart and *secret* soul of the sacred' (my emphasis).[21] But for those who discuss the state as the best means to prevent violence, legitimacy requires consciousness of what one is doing. This is an important difference, and we shall return to it.

Revivals and Apocalyptic (Messianic) Doctrines

Our fourth reason for associating religion and violence is based on what the concept of religious revival seems to entail. For Girard, primitive religions inevitably develop 'crises' where the sacrifices are neglected. Each particular crisis is resolved when the outbreak of primordial violence brings home again the significance or utility of the sacrificial rite. In this, Girard reminds us of Machiavelli, perhaps the first to stress the extraordinary kinship between religious and political communities, who noted that if you want to preserve a state, study religions which know how to go back to their 'first principles'.

> And those are the best-constituted bodies and have the longest existence which possess the intrinsic means of frequently renewing themselves, or such as obtain this renovation in consequence of some extrinsic accidents. And it is a truth clearer than the light of the sun that without such renovation, these bodies cannot continue to exist; and the means for renewing them is to bring them back to first principles. For, as all religions, republics and monarchies must have within themselves some goodness, by means of which they obtain their first growth and reputation, and as in the process of time this goodness becomes corrupted, it will of necessity destroy the body unless something intervenes to bring it back to its normal condition. Thus, the doctors of medicine say, in speaking of the human body, that 'every day some ill humors gather which must be cured'.[22]

Khachig Tololyan's studies of the history of Armenian terror demonstrate the salience of Machiavelli's point concerning the similarity of the renewal process in religious and political communities. In fact, Tololyan develops the thought further, arguing that the original religious conceptions of a community can be used to revive a society which has become secular.

Specifically, Tololyan distinguishes some communities as depending upon paradigmatic texts to provide models for interpreting the world and acting in it. The Armenians have such a community, one which was originally built around a church, whose traditions and narratives cluster around the story of the fifth-century Armenian Saint Vartan and his thousand soldiers who lost their lives resisting odds they knew were hopeless. Renewals and struggles for leadership within the community since have been related to the ability to generate martyrdom and appropriate the particular symbols of the Armenian community associated with it. Viewed from this perspective, it seems reasonable to believe that although the Armenian terrorism during the past two decades has been largely directed against Turks, its true concern is to revive Armenian nationalism.

> It would be a mistake for analysts to delude themselves into believing, *as the terrorists themselves have*, that the true audience and target is Turkey and its NATO allies. Neither is likely to be moved; . . . The true audience of Armenian terrorism remains the Armenian Diaspora, whose fraying culture is constituted to a remarkable degree by old stories, and who see in contemporary terrorists Vartan's refusal to abandon cultural identity and national rights.[23]

The relationship between self-deception and truth here seems to differ from that suggested by Girard, because Tololyan concludes that unmasking the delusion in this particular case benefits the community. In any case, what participants believe they experience and the unconscious dimension of that experience are two legitimate but very different kinds of accounts. My concern for the rest of this article will be with that conscious level, with the renewer's wish to return to the explicit conceptions and life-style of those who established a particular community.

> Now with regard to religion we shall see that revivals are equally necessary, and the best proof of this is furnished by our own, which would have been entirely lost had it not been brought back to its pristine principles and purity by Saint Francis and Saint Dominic; for by their voluntary poverty and the example of the life of Christ, they revived the sentiment of religion in the hearts of men where it had become almost extinct.[24]

This process of going back to the source of 'goodness' or renewing the life energy of the community rekindles, Machiavelli thinks, the activism of believers who, otherwise, over the course of generations become passive. Whatever the logic of the process, the revivalist phenomena is certainly a major feature of many religions, particularly Judaism, Christianity, and Islam.[25]

What Machiavelli does not articulate fully (and this seems ironic given his own obsession with violence) is that in the revealed religions this generally means a renewed contact with the source of violence. For the origin of a religion is precisely the juncture where the struggle with violence was most profound, the point at which most of the central images and metaphors to which Juergensmeyer calls our attention were created.

Sometimes, the connections between revival, origins, and violence are obvious. No one can discuss the contemporary revival among the Sunni without referring to the renewed interest in earlier views of the jihad, of Muhammad, and of his first three successors – the early Caliphs. In early Islam jihad meant military struggle; Muhammad and his immediate successors were great warriors.[26] In Iran the martyrdom of Hussain at Karbala in Islam's first century which served as the incident to establish the Shiah faith has received extraordinary attention and new meaning in recent years.[27] In Israel today Gush Emunim members explicitly point to the extraordinarily ruthless character of the original conquest of Canaan. One can see, too, that early in the Exodus narrative, after the Egyptian army drowns in the Sea of Reeds, a striking new attribute of God is revealed in Israel's song of exultation – 'Yahweh is a warrior, Yahweh has covered himself with glory.' (Exodus, 15). The Sinai Covenant (the event which constituted Israel as a political community) was, *inter alia*, a partnership between God and Israel for the explicit purpose of taking the Promised Land, a war unique among the Israel's wars, just because it was the only war where God participated. In this war, the *herem* (the religious mandate to exterminate enemy populations and utterly demolish their possessions) was applied. Also, this war became the model for the Christian holy war (Crusades) as well as the Muslim jihad, although each used it in different ways for unique purposes.[28]

In their founding periods Islam and Israel are warrior states. But the origins of Christianity look very different. Just as Christ is seen as the innocent victim of violence and persecution, so the early Christians saw themselves as innocent sufferers for His sake. Until the fourth century, when Christianity became a state religion, most Christians were pacifists. Undeniably, the Gospels provide powerful justifications for pacifism, and the return to Christian roots normally produces pacifist movements.

Yet there are elements in early Christian experience which have led some groups in various periods to rather different conclusions. For returning to the vision of early Christianity can mean rediscovering how important Christian apocalyptic or millenarian expectations were then, expectations which generally visualized Christ returning with a sword, exacting revenge for the suffering of the saints, and producing a wholly new and cleansed world where human nature would be utterly transformed and perfected and history would be brought to an end.

> And I saw heaven opened, and behold a white horse; and he that
> sat upon him was called Faithful and True, and in righteousness he
> doth judge and make war . . . And the armies which were in heaven
> followed him upon white horses . . . And out of his mouth goeth a
> sharp sword, that with it he should smite the nations. . . . And I
> saw the beast, and kings of the earth, and their armies gathered to
> make war against him that sat on the horse, and against his army.
> And the beast was taken, and . . . cast into a lake of fire burning
> with brimstone. And the remnant were slain . . . and all the fowls
> were filled with their flesh.[29]

Medieval and early Reformation millenarians such as the Anabaptists
and Thomas Munzer found Christian texts of this sort associated with
the founding period useful vehicles to justify extraordinary kinds of
atrocities. And today in the most violent expressions of Latin American liberation theology, millenarian expectations, i.e., the 'Kingdom
of God', loom large. (It is not a coincidence that Engels regarded
Munzer's use of these millenarian themes as the first expression of
modern revolutionary doctrines,[30] and that Georges Sorel saw the
Christian millenarian expectations as a superb model for proletarian
violence.)[31] All Protestant groups in the Reformation, we should
remember, understood themselves to be returning to Christian roots,
and yet the Reformation was the scene of the most fearsome savage
upheavals.

While the acceptance of the Crucifixion is predominantly regarded
as an argument against violence, the Crucifixion also represents a
devastating experience with violence; and the Gospels themselves have
some ambiguity on what the role of violence should be. Certain passages
have always been useful to renewers rejecting the pacifist commitment.
Jesus' fury in cleansing the Temple is one, and a striking description of
his mission is another:

> Do not suppose that I have come to bring peace to the earth, it
> is not peace I have come to bring but a sword. For I have come
> to set a man against his father, a daughter against her mother, a
> daughter-in-law against her mother-in-law. A man's enemies will
> be those of his own household.[32]

The violence of the founding moment frequently involves action
against outsiders. It is also brought about because the creation of a
new community requires participants to cast out those who explicitly
support the old principles and to expunge that portion of themselves
which, despite their will, is influenced by previously existing sacred
commitments. This last demand is, of course, always the most difficult;

and it is precisely in the context of this demand that Jesus reminds his disciples not to expect peace 'but a sword'.[33]

In the call of a later generation to return to the source of the religion, a similar pattern can be observed. Only this time, instead of another religion, another interpretation of the founding moment which is being rejected – a process which is possible only because religions normally have conflicting, even 'contradictory', precedents. In Islam, for example, the separate phases of Muhammad's career have produced two different traditions. The younger Muhammad rebelled against the people, while the older person governed them; and, hence, only the renewers of Islam have traditionally found the rebel phase more compelling while the later phase attracts the majority of Muslims most of the time, especially among the Sunni.

The millenarian theme is a much more common one among Christian renewers, and it is possible, as I have suggested, to interpret Christ as a revolutionary political figure, one who justifies violence. To do this, however, other portions of the sacred text may have to be elevated to pre-eminent positions, which is why many liberation theologians have made Exodus the 'privileged text'.[34]

The renewer may in time find himself literally at war with the establishment or those who he charges have corrupted the religion, and the latter in turn will begin to believe they must respond in kind. Civil wars, like religious wars, are generally more brutal and more prolonged, and when a civil war is also a religious one, the horror is compounded, for one is obliged to pursue heretics and/or apostates in a peculiarly shocking manner.[35]

Millenarian (Messianic or apocalyptic) movements which anticipate that the world as we know it will be radically transformed into a condition of perfection are essential elements in Judaism, Christianity, Islam and Buddhism. Specifically, they are frequently associated with revivalist movements and that association is particularly striking today.[36] In Israel, for example, the pattern is quite obvious; the two leading and quite different fundamentalist elements, the Gush Emunim (Block of the Faithful) and the various Haredi (God-Fearing sometimes called ultra-Orthodox) communities are Messianists.[37] In Britain and America the driving force of Christian fundamentalism, Sandeen has shown us, is millenarianism.[38] 'Messianism has (always been) an essential feature of Shii Islam.' Its most visible expression is the 'innumerable examples (of armed insurrection) throughout the length and breadth of the Islamic world, and through centuries of Islamic history'.[39] It was a critical element in the recent Iranian revolution and has been an element of Shia political activity since. Millenarianism exists among some contemporary groups in Sunni Islam, but it is less significant here. Nonetheless, the concern with Islam's origins, which all Sunni revivalists have, is a concern with a period in which millenarian themes were very pronounced, perhaps more so than at any other time in the history of Islam.

Students of millenarian groups know them to be characterized either by an extraordinary militancy which drives some to 'force the end' or, by a refusal to participate in the existing political order. In the history of Christian Messianic groups, the first policy often led to terror, that is violence which goes beyond the accepted moral restraints limiting criminal and belligerent activity, and the second to pacifism.

Among the Jews two distinctly different types, similar to but not identical with those in Christianity, can be found. Those who believe that one can act to shape the Messianic process like the Gush Emunim are hyperactive in developing the Messianic intimations of the existing order, a zeal which has led some Gush leaders to organize the two major Israeli terrorist enterprises against Palestinians in recent years: the 'Jewish Underground' and the 'Temple Mount Plot'. The Haredi, who believe human efforts to shape the Messianic process to be presumptuous and sinful, move precisely in the opposite direction. In effect they withdraw from the Jewish State whose legitimacy they do not recognize. They do occasionally participate in legal and illegal acts, normally to prevent Jews around them from flagrantly violating sacred laws.[40]

Throughout their history the Haredi urge what at first glance seems to be a virtually complete submission to the power of the Gentiles, and in this respect they simply exaggerate the propensity of the traditional Jewish doctrine and behavior during the Diaspora.[41]

> They (the Zionists) have abandoned the Jewish paths of submission (hachna'ah). It has become a contemptible word. Struggle and revenge are perceived as heroism and idealism. Jews in all times cautiously heeded the oath of our blessed sages not to rebel against the nations . . . It often happened that Jews let themselves be killed even by a far weaker adversary because they thought that victory would prove costly for the Jewish people as a whole. But the new times produced new leaders who called for a physical struggle and who are envious of nations that sanctify war, which is entirely unsuitable for the Jewish people.[42]

> The Jewish people was (sic) led to the slaughter 'as sheep to the slaughter shall be led' even when they had the strength to fight back

so that their enemies would not take revenge on our Jewish people elsewhere. *For this is a greater honor for the Jewish people than suicide by means of an uprising without any hope for the victory of life.* (emphasis added)[43]

They learned from generations of exile to bow their heads before every wave and to throw some money and some honor at their feet in order to preserve their life which is worth all the money and all the honor in the world, where there was no other way to save their souls.[44]

But there were clear limits to Haredi submission; when called upon to deny their faith, they accepted martrydom (kiddush hashem), a martrydom which often generated a strikingly heroic order of non-violent activities. On those occasions when the Haredi sanction violence, it is very limited and directed almost exclusively against Jews seen as 'desecrating' the 'traditionally orthodox way of life', thus placing the community as a whole in jeopardy.[45]

Islam has produced its own version of these two types. The entire Shiah religious community at irregular intervals moves from passive to active phases, the latter usually being accompanied by violence. Particular Sunni millenarian sects often develop a similar rhythm.[46] In its most extreme form, the passivity of the Shi'ah is justified by the extraordinary doctrine of *taqiyya* which not only permits submission to powers deemed illegitimate but also allows the denial of one's true religious beliefs, a conception wholly alien to Judaism and Christianity.

Within Christianity, as indicated, the alternation of active and passive phases is often associated with pacifism and terror. But it need not be. Christian fundamentalists in America have never been pacifists even when they eschewed politics in their initial phase (from the 1860s to the 1950s). Only recently have they become active;[47] and although virtually all rejected violence, a phenomenon unprecedented in the history of American fundamentalism, several terror groups appeared on its fringes.[48]

How does one explain these two different patterns, the tendency to withdraw from the larger society and the propensity to become extraordinarily active in it? Why do some communities and sects alternate from one phase to another, sometimes more than once?

My own sense is that the postures often reflect two different judgments about time. Groups that have withdrawn are waiting for the Messianic process to begin, while the exceedingly active are convinced that the Messianic process has begun already.

Time

The Messianic preoccupation with time reminds us of a major theme in Emmanuel Sivan's elegant *Radical Islam*. He argues that a profound gloom pervades Sunni radicals and periphal groups concerning Islam's capacity to survive the power and appeal of modern secularism. Squabbles between radicals, and between the radicals and the mainstream, do not represent differences in values so much as they do differences in judgements concerning how much time is left.

> If urgency does not necessarily lead to violence (though in some case it would) it does, however, lead to a divorce from – and almost always to some sort of revolt against – present Muslim society and polity.[49]
>
> . . . The position (among radicals is) that the distinction between educational effort and violence is immaterial. Both are cures to a terrible malady, both are predicated upon a 'five minutes to midnight' evaluation of the state of Islam.[50]

The extent to which the contemporary revival (or any revival for that matter) of religion is defensive and fueled by desperation is not an issue I am competent to discuss, though I believe that this characterization accurately represents much of the contemporary scene. For animals and humans, as individuals or in groups, the will to fight is greatly intensified by the conviction that one is trapped and by the belief that existence is at stake. This is why states nearly always try to justify their wars as responses to aggression: as Americans we all know that the only war in which our country was united began at Pearl Harbor.

Less obvious and extremely neglected, but just as important for our purposes here, is what we might call the 'logic of time'. As Sivan suggests, time does not necessarily create values so much as it compels us willy-nilly to give existing values different priorities. In all of our individual and collective undertakings, the ability to imagine nearness to or distance from future events influences emotions and activities immensely. Even unimportant routine matters gain significance just because they are due, while important concerns can be put off or not absorb us when we know that there is plenty of time or do not know when the deadline will be. Sometimes, the very meaning of a phenomenon may be altered by time. The millenarian promise, for example, tends to buttress the existing order if we cannot place it in time; but the sense that it is imminent (or even that it can be predicted) will always disturb existing arrangements greatly.

When time is working against us because obstacles increase constantly, because we have little time to prepare, and because we have no time to repair mistakes, the impulse to become violent can be irresistible. Mannheim might have exaggerated the importance of studying the time sense, but for those interested in violence this is a subject worth thinking about. 'The innermost structure of the mentality of a group can never be as clearly grasped as when we attempt to understand its conception of time in the light of its hopes, yearnings, and purposes.'[51]

Conclusion

Once alerted to the bond between religion and violence, one perceives the connections so striking, so demonstrable, and so various, that it comes as a surprise to discover that Girard's book is the only systematic or theoretical account of that bond available. And even if one rejects Girard's explanation, one must still deal with the issue it addresses or explain the nature and rationale of this extraordinary connection.

Social scientists often stress that the state and violence are inseparable and, therefore, Girard's analysis resonates; the reasons he provides for making violence *the* core of religion are the same ones that we offer for linking violence to the state. Religion is generated to tame a violent chaos, and to achieve that end it must use a new or special form of violence.

Furthermore, states and religions are connected to violence in four other ways to which Girard only alludes, perhaps because he finds the deliberate and calculated use of violence less interesting. The first two uses of violence by religions and states are obviously when it is martialed against foreign communities and when it is employed to prevent domestic upheaval.

A third use of violence occurs when efforts are made to reconstitute the social order. Periodically, religions experience crises which sometimes can be surmounted through renewal or revival activities. The process is reminiscent of revolutions in the state except that a revolution introduces a new principle of legitimacy while a revival claims to regenerate corrupted and misinterpreted principles. Nonetheless, the effort to regenerate or to introduce constituting principles of 'goodness' or legitimacy often brings one face-to-face with the original source of violence. In principle, it is impossible to identify those conceptions of legitimacy completely with any established order, and therefore they are always potential weapons to overturn existing relationships. This is one way in which the double, somewhat paradoxical element which religions and states share manifests itself. Most of the time believers and the citizens identify with existing authorities, but since neither religions nor states began that way is it plausible to think there will never be reason to revert?

A fourth similarity is that those who use violence for political or secular ends have various reasons to find religion attractive. My discussion was an elementary one, designed mainly to suggest possibilities, possibilities I have not yet fully explored myself.

The state, of course, is distinguishable because of its claim to monopolize violence; and I suspect that claim is rarely if ever made by religions, or at least it seems clear that religions lack the administrative mechanisms to make a claim of this sort viable. Monopolies, however, are always dubious and wasting assets, because they intensify discontent and focus its direction towards the holder which, indeed, may be one reason, and a rather substantial one, why religions are generally more durable than states.

NOTES

1. As far as I can tell, the frequency of wars justified on religious grounds has not been systematically studied. Richardson has some interesting material, and although his statistics are incomplete and confusing, they do indicate that only territorial claims exceed religious quarrels as a cause for war.

   As one might expect, there are differences between the statistics for different religions. Christianity and Islam seem more warlike than the Eastern religions, both with regard to other religions and internal concerns. Surprisingly, Christianity seems the most warlike. See David Wilkinson's interesting analysis of the Richardson data, *Deadly Quarrels: Lewis F. Richardson and the Statistical Study of Wars* (Berkeley, CA: University of California Press, 1980) particularly pp.87–91 and 112.

2. Ninian Smart, 'Religion, Myth, and Nationalism', in Peter Merkl and Ninian Smart (eds.), *Religion and Politics in the Modern World* (New York, NY: New York. University Press, 1983), p.23.

3. David C. Rapoport, 'Fear and Trembling: Terror in Three Religious Traditions', *American Political Science Review*, Vol.78, No. 3, (Sept. 1984), p.659. Obviously, the character of the violence, or the form of the assaults and the type of targets chosen will be affected too.

4. Bruce Hoffman, 'The Contrasting Ethical Foundations of Terrorism in the 1980s', *Terrorism and Political Violence* Vol.1, No. 3, (July 1989), pp.361–62.

5. As previously indicated there is no systematic study of this issue, but Quincy Wright's statistics show that in the West the intensity of the wars justified on religious grounds during the Reformation has been surpassed only by the wars of nationalities and ideology in the twentieth century. This conclusion confirms Toynbee's earlier assessment, Quincy Wright, *A Study of War* 2nd ed. (Chicago, IL; University of Chicago Press, 1965), p.256.

   Sorokin's index of war intensity, a weighted composite of five factors (duration, casualties, number of participating countries, and proportion of combatants) indicates that the religious wars of the seventeenth century were seven times more intense than those of the previous century and that the rate of increase was two to three times greater than that of any previous period. Wright, Table 49, p.655.

6. Leo Kuper, 'Theological Warrants for Genocide: Judaism, Christianity, and Islam', *Terrorism and Political Violence*, Vol.2, No.4 (Fall, 1990), pp.351–79.

7. Gerald Cromer cites the poem but not its name. '"In the Mirror of the Past": The Use of History in the Justification of Terrorism', *Terrorism and Political Violence*, Vol. 3 No. 4 (Winter 1991). Cromer argues that the religious references served autopropaganda purposes; that I'm sure is true, but it is also likely that the appeals were meant to persuade others too.
8. *Los Angeles Times*, 1 Oct. 1990, p.A6.
9. *Los Angeles Times*, 8 Sept. 1990, p.A6.
10. In my *Inside Terrorist Organizations*, (London: Frank Cass and New York, NY: Columbia University Press, 1988), pp.172–92.
11. 'There was a desire for death, and a need to live. To live in order to enter the court room – for this is the final chapter in the story of an active revolutionary.'
    'Your crown, *the crown of thorns*, is for all that the laurel wreath of the party, and to you too is due the credit for have bestowed upon the party a group of fearless martyrs' (my emphasis). Vera Figner and A.D. Mikhailov, *Narodnaya Volya* members cited by Zeev Ivianski, 'The Moral Issue: Some Aspects of Individual Terror', in my *The Morality of Terrorism*, 2nd ed., (New York, NY: Columbia University Press, 1989), p.240.
12. Khachig Tololyan, 'Martyrdom as Legitimacy; Religion and Symbolic Appropriation in the Armenian Diaspora', in Paul Wilkinson, and Alasdair M. Stewart (eds.), *Current Research on Terrorism* (Aberdeen: Aberdeen University Press, 1987), p.91.
13. Marue Perinbaum, *Holy Violence: The Revolutionary Thought of Franz Fanon*, (Washington, DC: Three Continents Press, 1982).
14. Bernard Lewis, 'The Return of Islam', in Michael Curtis (ed.), *Religion and Politics in the Middle East* (Boulder, CO: Westview Press 1986) pp.15–16. Lewis provides another (but not mutually exclusive) explanation for *Fatah*, i.e., a reversed Arabic acronym for the liberation of Palestine.
    One could argue that since Muslims are not supposed to fight Muslims, the only glorious victories the PLO could commemorate would be against non-Muslims, but then this contention only makes Lewis' point more forcefully.
15. Mostafa Rejai with Kay Phillips, *Leaders of Revolution*, (Beverly Hills, CA: Sage, 1979) p.72. Data is available for only fifty cases. Other high correlations are 95 per cent had legitimate birth, 94 per cent were members of revolutionary organizations, 80 per cent belonged to the religious majority, 63 per cent were of the ethnic majority, 53 per cent came from the middle class.
    One should note, too, that while nearly half became atheists no example of a Muslim abandoning his religion exists.
16. The sacrificial rite, Burton Mack points out, is at the heart of all primitive religions, and a credible theory of sacrifice will thus lead to 'a comprehensive account of social formation, religion, and culture, 'Introduction: Religion and Ritual' in Robert G. Hamerton-Kelly (ed.), *Violent Origins: Walter Burkert, René Girard, and Jonathan Z. Smith* (Stanford, CA: Stanford University Press, 1987), p.7.
17. René Girard, *Violence and the Sacred*, trans. Patrick Gregory (Baltimore, MD and London: The Johns Hopkins University Press, 1977) p.55.
18. Ibid., p.92 (Girard's emphasis).
19. Ibid., p.23.
20. Girard, of course, is discussing primitive religion, the religion of those who lack judicial institutions and must cope with violence by means of the blood feud. But in James A. Aho's examination of holy war conceptions in various highly developed religions he concludes that they did serve to keep 'anomie at bay' in the communities which sponsored them. *Religious Mythology and the Art of War*, (Westport, CT: Greenwood Press, 1981), pp.9–11, 23, 30, 218.
21. Ibid. p.31.
22. *Discourses*, Vol.III, No.1.
23. 'Cultural Narrative and the Terrorist' in my *Inside Terrorist Organizations*, p.232, (my emphasis).

24. *Discourses* Vol.I, No.1. For conceptual purposes I have exaggerated the element of consciousness here. While Machiavelli believed that St. Francis and St. Dominic were consciously trying to revive Christianity, it is also true that he knew (while they did not) that ultimately nothing would really change. 'They continued to live in poverty; and by means of confessions and preachings they were able to make them understand that it was proper even to speak ill of wicked rulers, and that it was proper to render them obedience and to leave the punishment of their errors to God. And thus these wicked rulers do as much evil as they please, because they do not fear a punishment from what they do not see or believe.' Ibid.

25. Bernard Lewis believes that the activist-quietist cycle dominates the history of Islam. See 'On the Revolutions in Early Islam', *Studia Islamica* XXXII (1970), pp.215–31 and 'On the Quietist and Activist Traditions in Islamic Political Writing', *Bulletin of the School of Oriental and African Studies* Vol.10, No.9 (1986) pp.141–47. For Tololyan, Judaism, Christianity, and Islam are examples of communities which depend upon paradigmatic texts.

26. Jihad literally means struggle or striving. Since the nineteenth century more and more Sunni thinkers have thought of it primarily as a spiritual quest. In the recent renewal of Islam, the earlier view has been revived where 'the overwhelming majority of theologians, jurists, and traditionalists . . . understood the obligation of jihad in the military sense and have examined and expanded it accordingly'. Bernard Lewis, *The Political Language of Islam*, (Chicago, IL: University of Chicago Press, 1988), p.72.

27. This is the central theme of Michael M. Fisher's fascinating book, *Iran: From Religious Dispute to Revolution*, (Cambridge, MA: Harvard University Press, 1980).

28. *Herem*, refers to objects consecrated for sacred purposes and with which contact is forbidden because of their corrupting nature (Lev. 27:28 and Deut. 7:26). Israel's war of conquest was unusual, perhaps unique in its time, for most wars then aimed at making the enemy slaves and his goods booty. The Bible makes clear that Israel refused to apply the ban consistently. It is interesting to note that both the Israelite participants in the war as well as the enemy were considered under the *herem*, thus illustrating the double nature of the sacred.

29. Revelation 19:5.

30. 'The Book of Revelation' and 'On the History of Early Christianity', in Marx-Engels, *On Religion*, (Moscow: Progress Publishers, 1975) pp.180–86 and 275–302.

31. Georges Sorel, *Reflections on Violence*, trans., T.E. Hulme and J. Roth (New York, NY: Collier, 1981), pp.6ff.

32. Matt. 10:34. Ephiram K. Mosothoane's careful examination of the issue observes that while the Gospels do not condone violence, 'they vary in that the greater the intensity of the violence a Christian community suffered, the more inclined it was to wish its persecutors at least a taste of what it had suffered'. 'Violence and the Gospel Tradition', *Theology and Violence: The South African Debate*, ed. Charles Villa-Vicencio (Johannesburg: Skotaville, 1987), p.125.

33. The traditional, and I believe correct, interpretation of this passage, of course, is that the sword will be used against Christians because of the radical nature of their commitment.

34. The term 'privileged text' comes from J. Andrew Kirk, *Liberation Theology* (Atlanta, GA: John Knox Press, 1979), p.96. Liberation theologians say they focus on the exodus 'because it is *the* archetypical event of Israel which became converted into the foundation . . . of all its laws and institutions, as well as its theological reflection'. p.104. For a fascinating attempt to make the Book of Joshua a model for liberation theology militancy, see Walter Brueggemann, *Revelation and Violence: A Study in Contextualization*, (Milwaukee, WI: Marquette University Press, 1986).

    During the 1960s there were also serious efforts by historians (as distinguished from theologians) to see Jesus as a Zealot or a political revolutionary. For an interesting early account of these efforts, see George R. Edwards, *Jesus and the Politics of Violence*, (New York, NY: Harper & Row, 1972).

35. In Islam 'the rules of warfare against the apostate are very much harsher than those governing warfare against the unbeliever. He may not be given quarter or safe conduct, and no truce or agreement with him is permissible. If captured, he is not a prisoner of war. He cannot become a *dhimmi* (protected person) nor can he even hope like other captives of the *jihad* to live on as a slave. The only options before him are recantation or death'. Bernard Lewis, *The Political Language*, p.85. Cf. my discussion of the apostasy allegation in the assassination of President Sadat, 'Sacred Terror: A Contemporary Case from Islam', in Walter Reich (ed.), *The Origins of Terrorism; Psychologies, Ideologies, Theologies and World Views* (Cambridge: Cambridge University Press, 1990), pp.103–30.

Religious wars between Christians generally are more concerned with heretics than apostates, because in Christianity doctrine is so critical. During the centuries of the Crusades, heresy was regarded as the 'most grievous sin and crime into which one could fall . . . a traitor to God himself . . . (The heretic) imperilled others by his words and example; medieval writers were fond of likening heresy to a loathsome and contagious disease'. Heretics were regularly burnt and if buried before their sins were discovered, their bones were exhumed and burnt. In war heretics had no rights, and together with those thought to have recanted only from fear, were regularly consumed in holocausts. No distinction was made between combatants and non-combatants nor often even between heretics and their children. Walter Wakefield, *Heresy, Crusade, and Inquisition in Southern France* (London: George Allen & Unwin: 1976) pp.18ff. and 135ff.

The Israelite who turned to other gods was subject to the *herem*: destruction by the sword. Exodus 22:19. During the Jewish Diaspora, excommunication was the only sanction, perhaps the only feasible severe one.
36. 'Messianic Sanctions for Terror', *Comparative Politics*, Vol.20, No.2 (Jan. 1988), pp.200–201.
37. In a very profound sense, Judaism has been a Messianic religion since at least the first century, but the Messianic imagination dominates all activity only at certain times and in particular groups.
38. Ernest R. Sandeen, *The Roots of Fundamentalism: British and American Millenarianism, 1880–1930* (Chicago, IL: University of Chicago Press, 1970).
39. Bernard Lewis, 'The Shi'a in Islamic History', in Martin Kramer (ed.), *Shi'ism, Resistance, and Revolution* (Boulder, Co: Westview Press, 1987) pp.29–30.
40. See Menachem Friedman's rich 'Jewish Zealots: Conservative versus Innovative', *Religious Radicalism and Politics in the Middle East* (eds.), Emmanuel Sivan and Menachem Friedman (Albany, NY: SUNY Press, 1990) pp.120–52. For a fascinating discussion of the efforts of Haredi groups to control the residential patterns in Jerusalem, see Roger Friedland and Richard D. Hecht, 'Rocks, Roads, and *Ramot* Control: The Other War for Jerusalem', *Soundings*, Vol.LXX11, (Summer/Fall 1989), pp.221–73.
41. See Nahum Glatzer, 'The Concept of Peace in Classical Judaism', in his *Essays in Jewish Thought* (University: University of Alabama Press, 1978), pp.36–47; Leslie J. Hoppe 'Religion and Politics; Paradigms from Early Judaism', J. T. Pawlikowski and Daniel Senior, *Biblical and Theological Reflections on the Challege of Peace*, (Washington, DC: 1984), pp.45–54; Andre Neher, 'Rabbinic Adumbrations of Non-Violence', in Raphael Loewe, *Rationalism, Judaism, Universalism: II Essays in Memory of Leon Roth* (London: Routledge & Kegan Paul, 1966), pp.169–96.
42. Rabbi Yosef Elihu Hankin, as quoted by Menachem Friedman, 'The Haredim and the Holocaust', *Jerusalem Quarterly*, No. 53 (Winter 1990), p.102. I am indebted to Friedman's penetrating discussion of this moral position as it is reflected in the current Haredi literature on the Holocaust.
43. Rabbi Hankin as quoted by Friedman, p.103.
44. Rabbi Michael Dov Weissmandel as quoted by Friedman, p.104.
45. Menachem Friedman, 'Religious Zealotry in Israeli Society' in Solomon Poll and Ernest Krausz (eds.) *On Ethnic and Religious Diversity in Israel* (Ramat-Gan: Bar

Ilan University, 1975), p.92. Friedman characterizes the activity as 'largely verbal violence, (which) may closely border on physical violence', Cf. Haim H. Cohn, 'Holy Terror', *Violence, Aggression and Terror*, Vol.1, No.2 (1987) pp.1–12.
46. Peter von Sievers, 'The Realm of Justice; Apocalyptic Revolts in Algeria', (1849–79) *Humaniora Islamica*, No.1 (1973) pp.147–60.
47. Timothy P. Weber, *Living in the Shadow of the Second Coming; American Premillenialism, 1875–1982*, enl. ed. (Grand Rapids, MI: Zonderwan, 1983).
48. Michael Barkun, 'Millenarian Aspects of "White Supremacist" Movements', *Terrorism and Political Violence*, Vol.I, No.4 (Oct. 1989) pp.410–34.
49. *Radical Islam; Medieval Theology and Modern Politics* (New Haven, CT: Yale University Press, 1985), p.84.
50. Ibid., p.113.
51. Karl Mannheim, *Ideology and Utopia* (London: Routledge & Kegan Paul, 1936) p.209.

A Response:
Reflections from the Perspective
of Mimetic Theory

RENÉ GIRARD AND MARK R. ANSPACH

The two of us both feel that we learned a lot from these essays, and we are both aware that our knowledge in most of the fields to which these articles belong is very limited. Our comments are not intended as an evaluation of them; they record the ideas, primarily theoretical, that the papers suggested to us. The theory to which we constantly refer, explicitly or implicitly, is the mimetic theory, of course, to which we both subscribe but with some significant individual nuances.

In the light of the papers published here, and also of others presented at the H. F. Guggenheim Foundation conference, it seems that everything labelled fundamentalism, regardless of the religious or political tradition it affects, is a reaction to the same kind of fear of undifferentiation, and the mimetic theory can contribute to a better definition and understanding of this fear as well as to an awareness of its long history. There are specifically modern features, no doubt, in contemporary fundamentalism that distinguish it from traditional religions, but there are also highly traditional features.

In the Indian Puranas, for example, history is divided into cycles of four ages, and the fourth is the *Kali Yuga*, or somber age, which prepares the final disintegration. It is described as the age in which brahmins cannot be trusted, classes mix with each other, and people follow foreign customs until their perversity leads them to ruin. But, in this Hindu cosmology, there is nothing new about such a state of affairs: all known human history falls within the *Kali Yuga*.

The Puranas are a typical rendition of perceptions and values which are present in most traditional societies. They all root the dissolving of culture, if not an apocalyptic end of the world, in a sinful undifferentiation of human relations in which we can recognize an incomplete portrayal of the mimetic-sacrificial crisis. There are also purely literary examples of this, the most splendid and powerful of which is Ulysses' speech on the demise of 'Degree' in *Troilus and Cressida*; see R. Girard, *A Theater of Envy: William Shakespeare* (New York, NY: Oxford University Press, 1991), Chapters 18–20.

In a mimetic crisis, religious and cultural differences are felt to be slipping away as a result of an invisible but omnipresent influence. All efforts to hold on to the remaining differences and to recapture the lost ones increase the tension and conflicts, which arise less and less with other groups grounded in 'similar' traditions and more and more with those who hold to the opposite attitude, those for whom the crisis is caused by the differences themselves and who think that salvation lies in doing away with them entirely.

It is impossible to discuss fundamentalism without taking into account the perspective of the fundamentalists themselves and the reasons they think they have for thinking the way they do. The problem with some recent studies is that they completely ignore the fundamentalists' own viewpoint. We greatly appreciated David C. Rapoport's observations on this subject.

It is an objective fact that, not only in our society but in the entire world, differences tend to dissolve and disintegrate as a result of religious, social and political evolution. This evolution is inseparable from technological development, but it is the result of factors too complex and too numerous to be discussed in this brief statement.

This evolution is regarded by some as the best thing that can happen to the human race while others see it as the worst. The first do their utmost to accelerate this evolution; the second try just as hard to arrest it. The reason why religious aspects are becoming paramount once again is the conviction that religion is more deeply rooted, more basic, more primordial even, than anything situated at the political or social level.

In our view our culture is indeed in the midst of a deepening mimetic and sacrificial crisis, but this has been true for centuries, at least since the Renaissance, and we feel alien to the two attitudes we have just defined because it seems to us that both of them mutilate, or suppress entirely, certain aspects of our historical experience – or rather, of the way we ourselves interpret this experience.

We feel that even though there are negative aspects to the modern experience that remain strikingly typical of the traditional mimetic crisis, strikingly similar to what the Puranas describe, and therefore likely to trigger a 'fundamentalist' reaction, there are also immensely positive aspects, some of which may be unique to the age that is called 'modern', and they make the fundamentalist views unacceptable.

Studies which regard fundamentalism as some kind of pathology remain inevitably superficial in our view. They take no account of the role that, for instance, viewing fundamentalists as pathological cases may play, paradoxically, in the growth of fundamentalism.

The articles by Emmanuel Sivan and Ehud Sprinzak treat their subject with more respect than an apparently neutral stance would. The reader perceives a touch of anger in their tone that is the truly human reaction when people we regard as responsible human beings do intolerable things or espouse intolerable opinions. This does not mean that we advocate anger as the attitude that will solve the dilemma of which perspective to adopt *vis-à-vis* the problems we are discussing. It simply means that this problem is very difficult and probably insoluble.

Indeed, we do not think that some middle-of-the-road position can be defined between the extremes of 'fundamentalism' and 'post-enlightenment rationalism' from the comfort of which one could criticize the two extremes in any fashion that could be called 'objective' or 'scientific'. But this does not necessarily mean that the attempt should not be made. Our history is open-ended precisely because it cannot be imprisoned in the categories of these two extremes.

Turning now to the detail of the articles, it may be worth clarifying a point made by Emmanuel Sivan on the several remarkable cases of convergence that he found between Jewish and Islamic religious radicals. The problem is how to explain the rarity of expressions of mimetic desire in this area.

Sivan rightly emphasizes that the primary struggle of the radicals is with perceived apostates within their own religious camp: the Muslim-Jewish conflict is secondary to them. Radicals on 'opposite sides' are so far apart that they are not apart, that they are not rivals for the same constituency.

On the other hand, it is not surprising to find a much clearer case of mimetic rivalry between Amal and Hizbollah, since, as Martin Kramer so forcefully shows, these two movements are competing for leadership of the same Lebanese Shiite community. Precisely because of the intensity of their rivalry, however, it would be surprising were Amal openly to hold up Hizbollah as an example to be followed, as the radical member of the Knesset cited by Emmanuel Sivan did with the distant enemy Khomeini.

Any deliberate imitation of a close rival is likely to be left unspoken as the sign of a shameful lack of self-sufficiency and as a damning acknowledgement of superiority on the part of the rival. Moreover, imitation is just as likely to be unconscious and not deliberate at all. The word 'unconscious', though, does not have the same implications here as it does in Freud. By 'unconscious', we do not necessarily mean 'repressed', but simply 'unwitting'. People locked in rivalry may well be oblivious to the ways in which they come to resemble each other.

In fact, unconscious mimetic rivalry operates, most of the time, as a desperate search for and espousal of views, attitudes, and actions antithetical to those of the model. It operates, therefore, as a search for independence that produces an impoverished opposite of the model's attitude. The improverishment means that the job of acting, thinking and desiring differently from the model is bungled. It looks superficially successful because it focuses on spectacular features of the model's behavior and ideas but, at a deeper level, imitation prevails.

The main reason, however, that the actual behavior and thinking of the antagonists are the same is the mimetic process itself, the way rivalry necessarily operates. The antagonists' behavior and even thinking are shaped by the requirements of their struggle, which forces them to mirror each other no matter how fervently they may desire to differentiate themselves; to borrow Shakespeare's expression from *Timon of Athens*, they become *confounding contraries*.

Ehud Sprinzak's compelling portrait of the late Meir Kahane and his ideology stands as a case study of mimetic doubling in the revenge process. Sprinzak usefully places Kahane's early development in the context of 1960s America, in which militant spokesmen for other causes set an example with their talk of becoming 'the executioners of our executioners'. In contrast, Kahane's theory of revenge appears new and unprecedented in the context of the traditional attitudes of Jewish activists to Gentile persecution.

But the precedent must be sought on the other side, since, as Sprinzak observes, Kahane promoted the 'Gentilization' of the Jew, imitating the very persecutors on whom he sought revenge. If Kahane seemed an actor in a classical Jewish tragedy, it was because of his larger-than-life obsession with what Susan Jacoby in *Wild Justice* calls 'the longest-running revenge tragedy of western civilization': the persecution of the people blamed for 'killing Christ' (New York, NY: Harper & Row, 1983, p.68).

Gentiles rationalized their attacks on Jews by accusing them of having attacked God. Kahane's revenge theory merely reverses the roles. Identifying God with His 'chosen people', Kahane accused the Gentiles of attacking God: 'When the Jew is attacked – it is an assault upon the Name of God!' Jewish vengeance becomes God's own revenge in the way Christian vengeance was supposed to have been. Moreover, just as medieval Christians 'firmly believed that the Jewish Diaspora was God's revenge for the sin of deicide' (Jacoby, pp.102–3), Kahane's theory holds the ending of the Diaspora to be God's revenge against the Gentiles.

Kahane echoes another tenet of the medieval Christian revenge theory, the notorious 'blood libel', when he hails Jewish dominion over the holy places of 'the Church that sucked our blood'. Just as the Church once accused Jews of draining Christian blood, Kahane accused the Church of draining Jewish blood. Unfortunately, his use of the mythic language of 'blood-sucking' obscures the crucial distinction between the mythical nature of the Gentile blood spilled by Jews and the reality of the Jewish blood spilled by Gentiles. Worse, his actions threaten to nullify this distinction by making the ritualistic spilling of Gentile blood by Jews a reality.

Unrestrained, as Sprinzak notes, by ordinary political considerations, Kahane's quest for revenge assumed religious dimensions. But did its lifting of traditional Judaic checks on violence also reverse the normal function of religious ritual, as Ehud Sprinzak concludes? Certainly Kahane sought to increase tensions with external enemies, and he may have raised the level of discord in Israeli domestic politics, too. Still, an answer to this question might ultimately require an analysis of cleavages already existing in Israeli society. Martin Kramer's paper suggests the possibility that violence directed outward can serve to keep internal tensions under control.

Comparison of Kramer's study of the interface of religion and politics with Sprinzak's yields interesting parallels between Kahane's religious innovation and the transformation of Lebanese Shiism. Where Sprinzak attributes to Kahane the aim of liberating Jewish vengeful impulses held in check by generations of Halakhic sages, Kramer writes that the Lebanese Shiite community is stripping away the layers of pious restraint over violence accumulated through time by its own theologians. Also a religious minority, Shiism, like Judaism, traditionally emphasized inner repentance rather than blood vengeance. When Hizbollah's leading cleric called on believers to abandon self-flagellation in favor of resistance to the foreigner, struggle against the self was, in Kramer's words, transformed into struggle against the other. What is reversed here is the direction in which the violence is channelled, the direction of the sacrifice.

Martin Kramer also makes an important point in showing how the 'self-martyring' operations blur the distinction between self-sacrifice and sacrifice by the group. In fact, groups that undertake ritual sacrifice often seek to impart a self-sacrificial dimension to it (for a discussion of consenting victims in myth and history, see the fifth chapter of *The Scapegoat*). The striking arguments marshalled by Hizbollah's leading cleric to minimize the difference between a willing death in battle and 'self-martyrdom' cast the former in a new light. By setting out to blur the distinction 'between dying with a gun in your hand or exploding yourself', he suggests how recruits – whether conscripts or volunteers – can be sacrificed in the guise of cannon fodder.

In a sense, then, the explicitly religious framing of military actions renders visible an aspect of warfare that can be found in the West as well. Martin Kramer is duly careful to avoid the danger underscored by Bruce Lawrence of demonizing Islam. Generally speaking, the object in focusing on sacrifice is not to stigmatize the 'other' for primitive savagery, but to uncover the continuity among many distinct varieties of violence, including those our own societies practice.

We are reminded of how Stanford anthropologist Renato Rosaldo came to terms with his discovery that the gentle Philippine tribesmen with whom he lived were headhunters. When he received his draft notice for Vietnam, his companions 'were more horrified at the news that I might become a soldier than I was at the news that they took heads': 'What appalled them morally and was utterly beyond their comprehension was the fact that one guy would get up there and tell his brothers, as they would put it, to move into the line of fire' (in *Violent Origins*, Robert G. Hamerton-Kelly ed., Stanford, CA: Stanford University Press, 1987, pp.253–55).

An obvious reason for the outbreak of fratricidal warfare in Lebanon is the collapse of the state. David Rapoport and Bruce Lawrence both discuss state monopolization of violence. Bruce rightly emphasizes that no treatment of Islamic violence should neglect the role of the state. Of course, the Iranian revolution stands as a reminder that independent forces can successfully overcome the security apparatus of the state even today. The outcome of any given rebellion may depend, as Bruce Lawrence says, on the relative weights of national and religious loyalties. A Third World 'state-nation' is more vulnerable if it lacks a solid base in nationalism – which, as Mark Juergensmeyer suggests, is in important ways similar to and therefore a potential rival for religion.

Religion is susceptible to manipulation as an ideological resource, as Bruce Lawrence indicates, but stirring up Islamic feeling is a dangerous game when tried by pro-Western regimes eager to find a rival for socialist-oriented national movements. Lebanese analyst Georges Corm recently reminded Western readers that it was the Lebanese state itself, hoping to contain the expansion of Marxist nationalism among Lebanese youth, that invited in Musa al-Sadr, the Iranian-born cleric behind the awakening of Lebanon's Shiite community described by Martin Kramer. In the same way, Sadat, who was ultimately killed by an Islamic extremist, banned Nasserian youth organizations from Egyptian universities while opening them to Muslim Brotherhood groups that his predecessor had prohibited ('Le casse-tête moyen-oriental: religion ou géopolitique', *L'Evénement Européen*, Vol. 8, 1989, pp.99–113). It is well to remember, too, that America's own anti-Soviet strategy has led to direct support for Islamic extremists in Afghanistan and largely motivated our longstanding flirtation with Khomeini.

In any event, the relationship between religion, nationalism, and the state is a complex one – and could well provide the subject of another conference! David Rapoport's paper includes some interesting remarks on the similarity of the origin of religion proposed by *Violence and the Sacred* to the origin of the state conceived by Hobbes and other political theorists. The transition from the state of nature imagined by Hobbes furnishes an especially strong parallel, since the opening situation of war of all against all is resolved by establishing 'unanimity minus one'.

In the mimetic theory, the solution is a war of all against one – the victim; in *Leviathan*, it is in effect a war of one against all, since the sovereign is the only one to retain the unlimited right to the use of force that exists in the state of nature. In fact, the sovereign is the only one to remain in the state of nature because he alone is not a party to the social contract. As it turns out, this aspect of Hobbes' thought experiment corresponds to indigenous conceptions of monarchy reflected in myths of what Marshall Sahlins in *Islands of History* calls 'the stranger-king': 'By his own nature outside the home-bred culture of the society, the king appears within it as a force of nature' (Chicago, IL: University of Chicago Press, 1985, p.78). Although king and victim may appear poles apart, they are both excluded from the social contract (see pp.81–84 of M. Anspach, 'Tuer ou substituer: l'échange de victimes', *Bulletin du MAUSS* 12, Dec. 1984).

Unlike classical social contract approaches, though, the mimetic theory dispenses with the assumption of rationality by positing a spontaneous mechanism. It is, after all, much easier to choose a victim than a sovereign. One may then envisage a gradual development from a divine victim awaiting sacrifice to a 'ruler' who, initially powerless in the manner of the Amerindian chiefs described by Pierre Clastres, in time acquired real power. Thus, it is perhaps not so much that the state emerges when religion can no longer do what it was designed to do – and we should be particularly wary of loaded terms like 'design' – but that the emergence of the state out of the religious matrix eventually diminishes the need for violence-reducing religious rites. For a good early discussion of how ritual institutions are transformed into political ones, see ̔A. M. Hocart's *Kings and Councillors* (first published in 1936 and reprinted by the University of Chicago Press in 1970).

Mark Juergensmeyer takes the question of religion, violence, and the state to another level by formulating it in terms of the tension between order and disorder. In recent years, theorists in many fields have been thinking in new ways about the relationship between these two concepts. Order contains disorder, but it also emerges spontaneously from it. For Jean-Pierre Dupuy, the mimetic theory is an example of this type of reasoning: religion contains violence – in both senses of the word 'contain' – having emerged spontaneously out of it. It might be appropriate for us to conclude by referring readers interested in this broader theoretical perspective to *Disorder and Order*, the proceedings of an international, interdisciplinary symposium held at Stanford in 1981 (edited by Paisley Livingston and published by Anma Libri of Saratoga, CA, 1984).

Index

For Product Safety Concerns and Information please contact our EU
representative GPSR@taylorandfrancis.com
Taylor & Francis Verlag GmbH, Kaufingerstraße 24, 80331 München, Germany